Shifting Sands

Pocket Essentials by Gordon Kerr

A Short History of Europe
A Short History of Africa
A Short History of China
A Short History of Brazil
A Short History of the First World War
A Short History of the Vietnam War
A Short History of India
A Short History of the Victorian Era
A Short Introduction to Religion
The War That Never Ended
A Short History of Coffee
British Traitors
War Without Mercy

Shifting Sands

A **Pocket Essential** History of the Middle East

Gordon Kerr

Oldcastle Books

This new edition first published in 2025.
First published in 2016 by Oldcastle Books Ltd., Harpenden, UK
www.oldcastlebooks.co.uk
Editor: Nick Rennison

© Gordon Kerr 2016, 2025

The right of Gordon Kerr to be identified as the author of this work has been
asserted in accordance with the Copyright, Designs and Patents Act 1988.

All rights reserved. No part of this book may be reproduced, stored
in or introduced into a retrieval system, or transmitted, in any form
or by any means (electronic, mechanical, photocopying, recording
or otherwise) without the written permission of the publishers.

Any person who does any unauthorised act in relation to this publication
may be liable to criminal prosecution and civil claims for damages.

A CIP catalogue record for this book is available from the British Library.

NO AI TRAINING: Without in any way limiting the author's and publisher's
exclusive rights under copyright, any use of this publication to 'train' generative
artificial intelligence (AI) technologies to generate text is expressly prohibited.

ISBN
978-0-85730-616-6 (Paperback)
978-1-84344-637-8 (epub)

2 4 6 8 10 9 7 5 3 1

Typeset in 12 on 13.65pt Perpetua
by Avocet Typeset, Bideford, Devon, EX39 2 BP
Printed and bound in Great Britain by CPI Group (UK) Ltd, Croydon CR0 4YY

The manufacturer's authorised representative in the EU for product safety is
Easy Access System Europe, Mustamäe tee 50, 10621 Tallinn, Estonia
gpsr.requests@easproject.com

'Borders are the scars of history'
Robert Schuman, French statesman

Contents

Introduction	9
Ancient Civilisations	13
Christianity and Islam	33
External Threats	39
The Middle East to 1800	47
The Ottoman Empire After 1800	57
A New Middle East	77
The First World War and the Fall of the Ottoman Empire	91
Between the Wars	101
The Second World War	127
The Modern Middle East	131
New Threats	173
Index	217

Introduction

The Middle East describes a huge arc that encompasses Turkey, Iran, Syria, Iraq, Jordan, Israel, the Palestinian Territories, the Arabian Peninsula and Egypt. In fact, as a descriptive for this most ancient of regions the term 'Middle East' is of fairly recent coinage. Before the First World War, people were more likely to use the words 'the Near East' to describe the area that comprises Turkey, the Balkans, and the Levant (roughly the eastern Mediterranean – Cyprus, Israel, Jordan, Lebanon, Palestine, Syria and the Hatay Province of Turkey). When the term 'Middle East' was used at that time, it referred to Arabia, the Gulf, Persia, Mesopotamia and Afghanistan. This usage changed, however, with the defeat of the Ottoman Empire in the First World War which gave the Allies control of the empire's former Arab conquests. The term 'Middle East' gradually began to encompass both regions. The Second World War increased this usage, particularly as the entire region was treated as one strategic theatre of war by the Allies.

It is a term that is entirely Eurocentric, of course, and to people of the Indian sub-continent, for example, the region is really the Middle West. But, the West is now dominant in world affairs and is able, therefore, to look upon the world as if it were its own. It was not always thus, however. Only in the last five centuries have the nations of Europe and the West ruled the roost. For the four and a half millennia prior to that – the period of recorded human history — it was not the West, but the Middle East that took centre stage and played a leading role in the advancement of humankind.

So much of human history was created in the region now known as the Middle East, developments that have led to our own modern civilisation. One of the earliest surviving codes of law was compiled by the king of Babylon, Hammurabi (r. c. 1792-50). Akhenaten, a pharaoh of ancient Egypt's Eighteenth Dynasty abandoned polytheism for the monotheistic worship of Aten, thereby inventing the notion of the single, all-powerful deity. The oldest inhabited towns on earth, ancient settlements such as Jericho and Byblos, can be found there and the great religions of Islam, Judaism and Christianity have their roots there.

The Middle East has played a huge part in history and still does to this day. Its empires occasionally stretched into Europe. For instance, the Moors of the Umayyad Caliphate captured almost all of the Iberian Peninsula in the eighth century and Muslims controlled that part of the world until the thirteenth. The Ottoman Empire between the fourteenth and the seventeenth centuries extended its territory not only in the Middle East but also almost as far as Vienna. And, of course, there was European involvement in the Middle East before those times, with Byzantine and Roman possessions and cultural influence in the region.

After relative calm and stability under the Ottomans for a number of centuries, the twentieth century brought turmoil to the Middle East with interference from France and Great Britain who had their own imperialist agendas and with age-old religious and ethnic rivalries rising to the surface. We are still experiencing the fall-out from these and it appears that the situation is unlikely to change in the near future.

It is almost impossible to write a *short* history of this complex region with its web of rivalries and suspicions, but hopefully

INTRODUCTION

Shifting Sands: A Pocket Essential History of the Middle East will go some way towards unravelling these complexities and explaining how we arrived at the fragile situation of today.

Ancient Civilisations

The Middle East occupies a unique position in the history of humankind. It was probably in that area that, around 8,000 years ago, we first began to cultivate food crops and domesticate certain animals after perhaps a million years of subsisting on wild vegetables and hunting. It was this development, the result of a great deal of trial and error, that led to the advancement of human civilisation. Soon, great civilisations were appearing that would wax and wane throughout history up to the present day. They overlapped and interacted, often going to war with one another, their peoples merging and interbreeding through the centuries.

The first evidence of people becoming sedentary and beginning to establish urban centres has been found in the Mesopotamian Basin. This area, the name of which means 'land between rivers' (the Tigris and Euphrates), is home to many of the world's oldest major societies and is often described as the 'cradle of civilisation'. The first cities in history developed here during the Chalcolithic period of the Bronze Age from round about 5300 BC.

The Sumer and the Akkadian Empire (c. 5300-1700 BC)

First signs of the Sumerian civilisation, one of earth's oldest, can be dated back to roughly 5000 BC. The Sumerians are believed to have migrated to Mesopotamia from the areas of modern-day Turkey and Iran although there is no real certainty about this. One and a half thousand years later they had built cities in the Fertile Crescent, the area between the Tigris and Euphrates that provided the means to live in what was essentially a desert. Sumer became divided into a dozen or so independent city states each of which surrounded a temple dedicated to a god or goddess. The earliest city in Mesopotamia and, therefore, the oldest city in the world, is said to be Eridu in southern Mesopotamia. Four other cities were built before, it is suggested, being wiped out by a great flood which may be no more than myth.

These first cities came under the control of the Akkadian Empire between the twenty-fourth and twenty-second centuries BC. This empire was founded by Sargon the Great (r. c. 2334-2279 BC) who led his forces in the conquest of the Sumerian city-states. Sargon's empire grew to incorporate not just large parts of Mesopotamia, but also parts of present-day Iran, Asia Minor and Syria. It was amongst the first multi-ethnic, centrally ruled empires in history.

The Akkadian language became the *lingua franca* of the Middle East, used in government and administration while the Sumerian language remained in everyday use and in literature. Even when Sumer was no longer a great power, its language continued to be used in schools in the later civilisations of Babylonia and Assyria, in the same way Latin would later be used in mediaeval Europe. As well as being the inventors of bureaucracy, the Sumerians were amongst the first people to use the wheel. There is evidence that wheeled vehicles were being used from the second half of the fourth millennium BC in Mesopotamia.

Following a period of decline between around 2193 and 2154, the empire collapsed after an invasion by a nomadic people from the Zagros Mountains known as the Gutians. The

Sumerian king, Ur-Nammu (r. 2112-2095 BC), finally drove out the Gutians and restored his own people's rule. This 'Sumerian Renaissance' was the last great period of Sumerian power. By this time, however, Akkadian-speaking Semites were beginning to increase their presence and power in the region. Competing local powers such as Isin, Larsa and Babylon started to dominate the southern part of Mesopotamia and Babylon would become increasingly powerful.

At this time there was also a shift in population to the north. In the south, agriculture was in decline due to poor soil resulting from the silting of the Mesopotamian Delta. This led to an almost 60 per cent population decline between 2100 and 1700 BC. Sumer eventually fell under the control of the Amorites, a Semitic-speaking people from ancient Syria. This 'Dynasty of Isin', as it is known in the list of Sumerian kings, ended with the rise to power of Babylonia around 1700 BC with the notable Hammurabi as its ruler.

The Babylonian Empire (1894-333 BC)

Babylon was a small and unimportant city when the Amorites came to power around 1894 BC but during the reign of the great king Hammurabi (r. c. 1792-1750 BC) it rose to prominence. It had been a minor city-state, dwarfed by other, older states but Hammurabi's father Sin-Muballit (r. c. 1812-1793 BC) began the expansion of Babylonian power with the conquest of Borsippa, Kish and Sippar.

When Hammurabi took the throne, the region was controlled by a number of local powers. Eshnunna ruled the upper Tigris River; Larsa controlled the river delta; and Elam, in the east, regularly raided and took tribute from the weaker states in the southern part of Mesopotamia. In the north was the formidable

Assyrian Empire with its colonies in Asia Minor. It had expanded into central Mesopotamia and the Levant.

Hammurabi reunited Mesopotamia, but his most important legacy was the code of laws known as the Code of Hammurabi. One of the first written sets of laws in history, it was carved upon a stele that was located in a public place in Babylon where everyone could see it. Later, it was discovered in 1901 in Iran and taken to the Louvre in Paris where it can now be viewed. The code consisted of 282 laws, inscribed in the Akkadian language on 12 tablets. Dealing with such things as theft, dishonest dealings, violence to others, financial transactions and relations between various social classes, it was invariably harsh in its punishments:

'8 – If any one steal cattle or sheep, or an ass, or a pig or a goat, if it belong to a god or to the court, the thief shall pay thirtyfold therefor; if they belonged to a freed man of the king he shall pay tenfold; if the thief has nothing with which to pay he shall be put to death.'

The Code of Hammurabi, King of Babylon (1904),
translated by Robert Francis Harper

Soon after the death of this great king his empire began to disintegrate. Nomadic people began to arrive – the Central Asian Hittites and Mitannians; the Elamites who settled in Chaldea to the east of the Mesopotamian Basin; the Aramaeans from the Syrian Desert and the Assyrians from northern Mesopotamia. The Amorites continued to rule a much-reduced Babylon for several hundred years more and a number of Neo-Babylonian empires and kingdoms emerged. The last Amorite ruler was overthrown by the Hittites following the 'sack of Babylon' in 1595 BC, although the Hittites soon moved on, leaving the Kassites to take control. The

Kassites – Babylon's longest-lived dynasty – ruled until 1157 BC when Elam conquered it and then a few years later it was retaken by the native Akkadian-Babylonian, King Nebuchadnezzar I (r. c. 1125-1104 BC). Eventually, in 627 BC, after a period of chaos and three centuries of Assyrian rule, the Chaldeans seized the throne, ruling until 539 BC and conquering Assyria in the north of the region and Syria as far as the city of Tyre.

In 539, Babylon was conquered by Cyrus the Great (r. 559-530 BC), ruler of the Achaemenid Empire (also known as the First Persian Empire). Cyrus claimed to be the legitimate successor to the ancient Babylonian kings and he was ruler of almost the entire civilised world at that time. In 333 BC, the Macedonian ruler Alexander the Great (r. 336-323 BC) captured Babylon and, ten years later, died there. It was then absorbed, along with Assyria, into the Seleucid Empire. At this time, a new capital, Seleucia, was constructed and Babylon became neglected. The Mesopotamian Basin was ruled by the Persians – under the Parthians and then the Sassanids – before the Arabs arrived in 640 AD. Once again, Mesopotamia became a centre of power.

Ancient Egypt (3100-30 BC)

The River Nile has been the lifeblood of Egypt for millennia, providing a fertile floodplain that allowed humans to develop a sophisticated centralised society. Around 120,000 years ago, it was the abode of nomadic hunter-gatherers but, as North Africa became increasingly arid, populations gravitated towards the Nile where they began to develop an agricultural economy. Chiefdoms emerged and bureaucracy was necessary to settle such matters as disputes over farmland. Soon, around 1.8 million people were living and working on the long strip of arable land alongside the river. At around the same time as the Sumerian-Akkadian civilisation was emerging in Mesopotamia, Egypt was entering the Early Dynastic Period that followed the unification of Lower and Upper Egypt around 3100 BC. A capital was established at Memphis from which the first pharaohs controlled the labour force and farming in the Nile Delta. They also brought in revenue from the lucrative trade routes to the Levant that passed through Egypt. The pharaohs amassed great wealth which can be seen in the elaborate tombs that housed their bodies after death. This period established the institutions and system of centralised control that would help to create and maintain one of the greatest and longest-lasting civilisations the world has seen.

From 2686 until 2181 BC, the period known as the Old Kingdom, there were great advances in technology, as well as in art and architecture. Some of the enduring achievements of Ancient Egypt were created, such as the pyramids at Giza and the Great Sphinx. Agricultural yields were increased with coordinated irrigation networks. Both the construction of irrigation systems and the building of the pyramids were the work of vast numbers of peasants, conscripted into these ambitious communal projects. Meanwhile, a justice system maintained law and order. After around five centuries, the Old Kingdom collapsed under economic pressures leading to a period of turmoil during which the pharaohs' power greatly diminished and was challenged by regional governors. The First Intermediate Period – 2181 to 1991 BC – brought famine and civil war. Control of parts of Egypt was seized by local rulers and the country was split in two, rulers in what became Herakleopolis controlling Lower Egypt, and Upper Egypt being ruled by the Intef family in Thebes. Eventually, the Theban rulers came out on top and Egypt was once again unified.

The success of the Intef rulers and the beginning of the Twelfth Dynasty signalled an economic and cultural renaissance with land reclamation and irrigation projects being undertaken. Valuable territory in Nubia was recaptured and in the Eastern Delta, the Walls of the Ruler fortification was constructed by Amenemhat I (r. 1991-1962 BC) to protect Egypt's eastern approaches. Literature flourished and portrait sculpture soared to new levels of sophistication and detail.

The Second Intermediate Period, from 1674 to 1549 BC, brought a gradual decline in Egyptian fortunes and a Semitic Canaanite people, the Hyksos, seized power, forcing the government to flee to Thebes. The pharaoh was obliged to pay tribute to the Hyksos but Ahmose I (r. *c.* 1539-1514 BC) finally drove them from the country. The pharaohs of the New Kingdom (1549-1069 BC) fostered a period of prosperity and security and the empire grew to its greatest extent, stretching from Niya in the northwest of Syria to the fourth waterfall of the Nile in Nubia. Great construction projects included the temple at Karnak, the largest of all Egyptian temples. There were great pharaohs too – Hatshepsut (r. 1473-58 BC), one of the few women pharaohs, Akhenaten (r. 1353-36 BC) and Ramesses II 'the Great' (r. 1279-13 BC). Ramesses is recorded as having signed the first known peace treaty, with the Hittites after the indecisive Battle of Kadesh in 1274 BC. Following this battle, reluctant to engage with the powerful Middle Assyrian Empire, Egypt withdrew from Western Asia. Southern Canaan was lost to the Assyrians and corruption and civil unrest became rife.

The start of Egypt's Third Intermediate Period was dominated by the High Priests of Amun at Thebes who had little respect for the pharaoh. At the same time, Berber tribes from the area of modern Libya settled in the western Nile delta and began to carve out autonomy for themselves. The Libyan Berber or Bubastite dynasty ruled for two centuries. In 727 BC, King Piye (r. 752-21 BC) of Kush – in what is now the Republic of Sudan

– conquered Egypt, establishing the twenty-fifth dynasty. The country was reunited and restored to its former glory with a resurgence of the arts and architecture. In 671 BC, however, the Assyrian king Esarhaddon (r. 681-69 BC) invaded and brought the Kushite Empire to an end. Egypt was free of Assyrian vassalage by 653 BC but, in 525 BC, it was conquered by Persian king Cambyses II (r. 530-522 BC). In 332 BC, the Persians ceded Egypt to Alexander the Great and after Alexander's death, one of his generals, Ptolemy I (r. 323-283 BC), was appointed satrap of Egypt. He proclaimed himself king in 305 BC, viewed by Egyptians as the successor to the pharaohs. His family would rule until 30 BC. Alexandria became the capital and, with the famous Library of Alexandria at the centre, became a hub of learning and culture.

Egypt was of great importance to Rome which relied on its grain but as family feuds, rebellion and civil unrest destabilised the country, the Romans invaded to safeguard their grain imports. After Octavian – later Emperor Augustus – defeated Mark Antony (83-30 BC) and the Ptolemaic Queen Cleopatra VII Philopator (r. 51-30 BC) at the Battle of Actium, Rome made Egypt a colony, ruling through a prefect.

The Hittites (1650-1200 BC)

From around 1650 to 1200 BC, the Hittites dominated much of Anatolia (roughly modern Turkey) and the neighbouring regions. Their language was of the Indo-European family and they called their land Hatti. It is assumed that the Hittites arrived in Anatolia before 2000 BC, possibly from the Pontic-Caspian Steppe around the Sea of Azov in modern-day Ukraine. They either conquered or were assimilated into the native people who were already established there. They took time to integrate, initially living separately in various cities but before long strong leaders began to unite the various groupings of Hittite people, to conquer central Anatolia and establish the Hittite kingdom.

King Hattusili (r. c. 1586-1556 BC) is usually credited with founding the Hittite Kingdom, conquering territory to the north and the south of Hattusa — near modern Bogazkale in Turkey — which he made the capital of his kingdom. From this defensive stronghold he led his armies into the plains of Syria, campaigning in the Amorite Kingdom of Yamkhad. His son, Mursili I (r. 1556-26 BC) captured its capital, Khalpe (modern-day Aleppo) in 1595 BC. That same year, Mursili captured Mari (modern-day Tell Hariri in Syria) and Babylon. The strain placed on Hatti's finances caused by his campaigns brought strife at home, however, and on his return he was assassinated, his foreign conquests lost as Hatti dissolved into chaos. A period of weak rulers and inactivity ensued until, between 1400 and 1200 BC, centralised power and authority were re-established. Meanwhile, in the early fourteenth century BC, Hatti came under attack by the people known as the Gashga from the Pontic Alps to the north of the Hittites' territory. King Tudhaliya II (r. 1380-1360 BC) and his son King Suppiluliuma I (r. *c.* 1344-1322 BC) consolidated Hittite territory to the north and Hattusa was recaptured and fortified. Advances were made into Syria and there is evidence that the Egyptians began to accept the Hittites as their equals. Suppiluliuma's son Mursili II (r. 1321-1295 BC) expanded the empire.

In the thirteenth century BC, Muwatalli II (r. 1295-1282 BC) made Tarhuntasha his capital, moving the centre of power away from the threat of the Gashga. Control of western Anatolia was maintained and, in the Levant, a Hittite victory over an Egyptian army, led by Ramesses II, expanded the empire as far to the south as Damascus. During the reign of Tudhaliya IV (r. 1237-09 BC), however, the Assyrians began to raid the empire's eastern borders and captured territory from them in Syria. Finally, around 1200 BC, the empire began to disintegrate. The Hittite homelands became vulnerable to attack from every direction and in 1180 BC Hattusa was destroyed by a coalition of peoples – Kaskas, Phrygians and Bryges. The Hittite kingdom that had achieved so much was no more.

The Phoenicians (1550-300 BC)

The trading culture of the enterprising ancient Semitic seafaring nation of Phoenicia spread across the Mediterranean between 1550 and 300 BC. It was situated on the western shoreline of the Fertile Crescent along the coast of modern Lebanon, some of its cities reaching as far as the western Mediterranean. The Phoenicians' origins are unclear. The Greek historian Herodotus (c. 484-c. 425 BC) claimed that they originally lived on the shores of the Erythraean Sea – the ancient name for the northwest Indian Ocean. They migrated, he claimed, to the Mediterranean and started to embark on long voyages, bringing back goods from Egypt and Assyria. Whatever their origins, the high point of their culture and power was between approximately 1200 and 800 BC although many of their important settlements were already established by that time. This coalition of independent city-state ports was also linked to other ports on the Mediterranean islands and on other coastlines, making it ideally suited for trade between the Levant and the rest of the world. The most important of the trading posts the Phoenicians established on the Mediterranean coast was Carthage in modern Tunisia, established around 814 BC during the reign of Pygmalion of Tyre (r. 831-785 BC).

In 539, Phoenicia was captured, like most of the rest of the civilised world, by Cyrus the Great and was divided into four vassal kingdoms – Tyre, Sidon, Byblos and Arwad. Most

Phoenicians relocated to the city of Carthage. In 332 BC, following the Siege of Tyre, Alexander the Great captured the city, executing more than two thousand inhabitants. Macedonian dominance meant the end of the Phoenicians' control of Eastern Mediterranean trade routes and, although Carthage continued to prosper, Phoenician culture vanished in its homeland. Carthage was eventually destroyed by Rome in 146 BC at the conclusion of the Third Punic War. The Phoenicians were no more, but their legacy was the network of trading links that facilitated the transition from the prehistoric to the historic age.

Assyria (1250-612 BC)

In the second millennium BC, the city of Ashur, on the west bank of the Tigris River in northern Mesopotamia, was the hub of an extensive and highly lucrative trading network. It lay at the centre of the empire ruled by Shamsi-Adad I (r. 1813-1781 BC) that encompassed most of Mesopotamia, Syria and Asia Minor, an area sometimes known as the Kingdom of Upper Mesopotamia. Eventually, the empire began to fall apart and became vulnerable to attacks by the neighbouring powers of Yamkhad and Eshnunna. It went into decline during the next few centuries.

During the reign of Ashur-uballit I (r. 1365-1330 BC), Assyria's fortunes revived. He captured the rich farming lands of Nineveh and Arbela, north of Ashur and his conquests were consolidated by the rulers who followed him. Assyrian territory stretched from the Euphrates to the borders of the Hittite Empire. Under the warrior King Tukulti-ninurta I (r. 1243-1207 BC) it reached its greatest extent, his armies having defeated Babylonia to the south. He also founded a vast new royal complex across the Tigris from Ashur and named it Kar-Tukulti-Ninurta. Eventually, however, he was assassinated and his reign was followed by a succession of monarchs who ruled only briefly. The empire survived these setbacks and only Babylonia was lost but, by the end of the second millennium BC, the expansion of Aramaean pastoralist groups had resulted in the loss of a great deal of Assyrian territory.

It was not entirely the end of the Assyrians as a power in the region and, during the period known as Neo-Assyrian, from the ninth to the seventh centuries, they regained some of their former power under a series of exceptional leaders. They controlled all the major trade routes and were the most dominant state in the region, unequalled by any other in Anatolia, Western Iran, Babylonia or the Levant. Indeed, during the reign of Ashurnasirpal II (r. 883-59 BC), Assyria regained most of the territory it had lost several hundred years earlier.

Sennacherib (r. 704-681 BC) chose Nineveh as his capital and built what was known as the 'Palace without Rival' complete with a vast library. He captured Babylon and Lachish in Judah but was assassinated by two of his sons. Another of his sons, Esarhaddon (r. 680-69 BC) invaded Egypt, capturing Memphis in 671 BC, but died soon after.

For three centuries, Assyria battled to build and maintain its empire. At last, drained of wealth and manpower, lost in keeping the Medes, Scythians, Persians, Urartians and Cimmerians subjugated, the Assyrian Empire began to fall apart in the late seventh century BC. There were civil wars and rebellions and a force in which the Medes were predominant defeated them at Carchemish in 605 BC. This defeat marked the end of northern Mesopotamia as a political force.

Ancient Israel and Judah (Ninth Century-586 BC)

The first appearance of the name 'Israel' was on the stele of the Egyptian pharaoh Merneptah (r. 1213-1203 BC) – 'Israel is laid waste and his seed is no more'. It is likely that this Israel was a people living in the central highlands of Canaan and from the inscription it seems that it was a rival to Egypt's domination of the region. At this time, therefore, Israel contained a distinct ethnic grouping although archaeologists have struggled to discover really distinctive features that identify these people as distinctly Israelite. Surveys have revealed, however, the sudden emergence of a new culture during Iron Age I (1200-1000 BC) that is characterised by an absence of pork remains in contrast to other sites. Pork, for instance, formed 20 per cent of the diet of the Philistines. Pottery, too, was different, less decorated, and circumcision was practised. With no evidence of invasion or infiltration by a clearly defined ethnic group, it is surmised that the emergence of this new culture was an evolution from the existing culture. Around 250 hilltop settlements populated by the earliest Israelites suddenly appeared in the formerly sparsely populated region from the Judean hills in the south to the hills of Samaria to the north. Hebrew, until then merely a dialect of the Canaanite language, became the language of the area and later spread from the hill country to the valleys and the plains.

The Kingdom of Israel was characterised by its devotion to the god Yahweh, considered by the Israelites to be the only true god. It was a belief that rulers such as David (r. 1010-970 BC) and Solomon (r. 970-931 BC) used to unify the country. The Jews were different to the peoples who invaded and settled in Palestine and Syria in that they did not intermarry with other peoples or make efforts to become assimilated into the other peoples of the region. They devised one of the world's three great monotheistic religions, the Ten Commandments and the legal system derived from them, undoubtedly the most sophisticated moral system created until that time. They did not proselytise with their religion and it would not, therefore, generate the huge numbers of followers that the other monotheistic religions – Christianity and Islam – later enjoyed.

The kingdom split into two small Jewish states around 930 BC with the Kingdom of Israel occupying the northern part and the Kingdom of Judah the southern. Between 1000 BC and 550 BC, Israel flourished, its population expanded and trade prospered. By the second half of the tenth century BC, a state was consolidated with its capital at Samaria. In the eighth century, Israel was at war with the Neo-Assyrian Empire which, in 722 BC, destroyed Samaria. The Assyrians established control of the entire kingdom of Israel, deporting the inhabitants of Samaria to Assyria. Israel would not regain its status as an independent political entity until 1948.

The Jews enjoyed some autonomy during the Maccabean kingdom (166-63 BC) and under its successor, the House of Herod. A rebellion by the Jews against the Roman Empire in 70 AD led to the destruction of Jerusalem and in 135 AD their final revolt was quashed by the Roman Emperor Hadrian (r. 117-138 AD). After that, only a few thousand Jews were left in Galilee.

Meanwhile, the Kingdom of Judah, with its capital at Jerusalem, prospered during the reigns of rulers such as Omri (r. *c.* 876-869 or 884-872 BC), Ahab (r. *c.*871-852 BC) and the later dynasty of Jehu (842-746 BC), before becoming an Assyrian vassal state in the seventh century BC with control of the lucrative olive industry. When the Assyrian Empire disintegrated in the second half of the seventh century, however, Judah suffered at the hands of Egypt and the Neo-Babylonian Empires and was destroyed between 597 and 582 BC. This was followed, during the Babylonian period, by a decline in both economy and population as well as the loss of great swathes of territory to encroachments by neighbouring peoples. Jerusalem was greatly diminished from its former glory and the town of Mizpah in Benjamin became capital of a new Babylonian province that was named Yehud Medinata. In 539 BC, Babylon was conquered by Cyrus the Great's Persian army and Judah became part of the Persian Empire.

Achaemenid Empire (550-330 BC)

Also known as the First Persian Empire, the Achaemenid Empire was founded by Cyrus II 'the Great', the name Achaemenid coming from King Achaemenes who was said to have ruled Persia between 705 and 675 BC and to have been an ancestor of Cyrus. Despite its description as the First Persian Empire, the Achaemenid actually followed an empire created by another Iranian people, the Medes. They had risen to pre-eminence towards the end of the seventh century BC and the Persians became part of their empire, helping them to defeat the Assyrians.

Cyrus led his men in a rebellion against the Medes in 550 BC, defeating King Astyages (r. 585-550 BC) and uniting the Achaemenid kingdoms of Parsa and Ansan into one Persian state. A number of years later, the Lydian Empire, ruled by King Croesus (r. 560-547 BC), attempted to take advantage of the instability in the region, pushing eastwards and threatening Persian cities. In response, Cyrus led an army into Lydian territory, taking the Lydian capital, Sardis, and completing the conquest of the region in 546 BC. It was now the turn of the Babylonians and the Egyptians who had been allies of Lydia. By 540 BC, Cyrus had taken Elam and the following year routed the Babylonian army at the Battle of Opis. After capturing the city of Babylon itself, Cyrus proclaimed himself 'king of Babylon, king of Sumer and Akkad, king of the four corners of the world'. By the time of his death in 530 BC, he had created the greatest empire the world had ever seen, stretching from Asia Minor to northwest India.

SHIFTING SANDS

Cyrus's son Cambyses (r. 530-522) conquered Egypt in 525 BC and when Darius I 'the Great' (r. 522-486 BC) came to the throne, his empire included most of West Asia, Thrace-Macedonia and Paeonia in the Balkans, much of the regions bordering on the Black Sea, parts of the North Caucasus, and parts of north and northeast Africa, including Egypt, eastern Libya and the coast of Sudan. He brought stability, building roads to improve communication and introducing a system of governors, known as satraps. He added northeastern India to his vast territory and initiated the construction of royal buildings at Susa as well as the new capital of Persepolis. He spent the early years of his reign subduing rebellions in the empire and even travelled to Greece in an attempt to punish Athens and Eretria for helping rebels in Aeolis, Doris, Cyprus and Caria when they revolted between 499 and 493 BC. He was defeated at the Battle of Marathon in 490 BC but succeeded in re-conquering Thrace, Macedon, the Cyclades and the island of Naxos.

His son Xerxes (r. 486-465 BC) vowed to complete his father's work of forcing Sparta and Athens to acknowledge Persian superiority, but when they refused, he invaded Greece, winning the Battle of Thermopylae in 480 BC. Defeat at the naval Battle of Salamis, however, forced Xerxes to withdraw. The Persian army he left behind was finally defeated at Plataea and Mycale, encouraging the Greek cities to revolt and throw off the Persian yoke. Persia's European adventure was at an end.

During the reign of Artaxerxes II (r. 404-358 BC), Egypt declared independence from the empire. But around this time, Philip of Macedon (r. 359-336 BC) was uniting the Greek states in readiness for an invasion of the Persian Empire. In 334 BC, Philip's son, Alexander III 'the Great', carried out his father's plan by launching an invasion of Asia Minor. In 330 BC, the Persian Empire was added to Alexander's conquests.

Hellenistic Period

Alexander's death at the age of only thirty-two in June 323 BC in Babylon, signalled the end of his dream of a huge Hellenistic empire. His generals immediately began to quarrel and divide up an empire that stretched from Persia to Egypt. Ptolemy I (r. 323-283 BC) took over Egypt and founded the Ptolemaic Dynasty, lasting until 30 BC. Antigonus (r. 306-301 BC) took over Asia Minor, establishing the Antigonid Dynasty, lasting until 168 BC. Seleucus I Nicator (r. 306-281 BC), was given Mesopotamia and the Fertile Crescent and created his Seleucid Empire, lasting until 63 BC.

Two hundred years after the death of Alexander the Great, the Seleucids of Persia were deposed by the Parthians, a nomadic tribe from the region of the Caspian Sea. The Parthians persisted with the Greek method of government and the Greek language was still used as well as their own. Greek influence lasted until the first century AD. In Syria and Palestine, which had been conquered by the Syrians, the Greek influence lasted longer, especially in the north and west, on the Mediterranean coast. But to the east of Mount Lebanon, Greek influence diminished. In the Ptolemaic and Seleucid Empires, senior officials, civil servants, prominent businessmen and merchants, scholars and intellectuals were Greek, even though the Greeks remained a minority in both empires.

The Roman Empire

In 60 BC, after civil war and anarchy had devastated Rome, the triumvirate of Roman generals – Pompey (106-48 BC), Julius Caesar (100-44 BC) and Crassus (115-53 BC) assumed power. To Pompey was allocated the task of establishing the domination of the Roman Empire in Asia Minor and the eastern Mediterranean, work delayed in previous years by Rome's turmoil. He invaded Syria, capturing the important city of Jerusalem but a heavy defeat by the Parthians led to them holding Syria for a time. Only after the assassinations of Julius Caesar and Pompey, when the Emperor Augustus (r. 27 BC-14 AD) came to power, did the entire Middle East become part of the Roman Empire. The Parthians retained control of Persia and the area of present-day Iraq but Augustus wisely decided that peace should be fostered in the region so that Rome could consolidate its vast new territories.

So the Roman Middle East settled down to several centuries of Pax Romana and all that implied – good government, efficiency and an effective justice system. Tax was raised and the Romans built and improved roads and communications. Egypt became a very important base for Roman troops and was one of the most important exporters of food to the capital. Meanwhile, security was increased and maintained by the Roman legions. The Red Sea was cleared of the pirates who had been damaging trade and was re-established as an important artery for trade with India. In Egypt, peace came at a price because it was ruled with an iron fist, and suffered a heavy tax burden. Despite this, its Greek elite went along with Roman rule, cooperating fully and being allowed to retain their status. Ever flexible, the Romans treated Syria a little more leniently. Local rulers in the eastern, or 'Semitic' part of the region were permitted to retain their autonomy in return for a curbing of their ambition and they would be swiftly dealt with if they became a threat to the more settled peoples of the west.

A more direct form of rule was applied in the western or Mediterranean region of Syria. Its population was a mix of Mediterranean and Semitic, the Greeks having been a powerful presence here in cities built during the time of the Seleucids.

Their educated urban population was a good fit with Rome and many obtained Roman citizenship. There were many hugely successful Syrian doctors, lawyers and administrators and they were pre-eminent in the arts as well. Syria also provided several Roman emperors later in the history of the empire. Two of them – Caracalla (r. 198-217) and Elagabalus (r. 218-22) – have gained notoriety as two of the worst and cruellest emperors, although in 212, it was Caracalla who made the decision to grant Roman citizenship to the entire Roman Empire. A slightly better example of an emperor from Syria was Philip 'the Arab' (r. 244-249).

There was always tension, of course, and nowhere was this worse than in Palestine. Herod (r. 37-4 BC) was appointed King of Judaea by the Roman Senate and succeeded in conquering most of Palestine, becoming known, consequently, as Herod 'the Great'. He was an Arab but followed the Jewish religion and during his reign did much for the Jews such as rebuilding the Temple of Jerusalem. However, he was hated because of his connection with Rome and has become vilified in the Christian religious tradition because of his slaughter of the innocents at Bethlehem and because Jesus Christ was born, preached and was executed in his kingdom.

Christianity and Islam

The Rise of Christianity

Jesus and his Apostles were Jewish and Christianity was originally a movement within the Jewish religion. It was not taken up by Jews in general, however, and began, instead, to be embraced by non-Jews, or gentiles. It began to appeal to the poor and underprivileged people of the Graeco-Roman world and not even horrific persecution could prevent its rapid spread. It first arrived in Egypt with St Mark (?-c. 68), sometime after the death of Christ and took off amongst ordinary Egyptians. Meanwhile, the Greek elite maintained their worship of pagan gods.

In Rome, the old religions – especially the cult surrounding whoever was emperor – remained firmly in place for another three centuries, persecution coming and going on the whim of the emperor. Nonetheless, there were Christians at all levels of society. The religion even penetrated the ruling class, the imperial family and Rome's aristocrats. As it increasingly gained ground, Emperor Diocletian (r. 284-305) instituted a wave of terrible persecution but his successor, Constantine the Great (r. 306-337), declared himself converted and proclaimed Christianity the official religion of the Roman Empire. Of course, Constantine may have been merely acknowledging Christianity's growing popularity and accepting the inevitability of its increasing domination and, indeed, the religion was here to stay, its success possibly helped by the decline of an empire beset by internal strife between rival emperors and cross-border attacks by Goths and Persians.

The Rise of Islam

Born in western Arabia, the Prophet Muhammad (c. 570-632) created one of the great religions, now practised by around 20 per cent of the world's population. Muslims view the Prophet as the last of God's messengers, following Moses and Jesus Christ. To Muslims, therefore, Islam is the ultimate faith, completing and perfecting the work of the two prophets who came before him. But, it must be remembered that Muhammad is considered to be merely a messenger; he is not divine. Islam is the most determinedly monotheistic of the world's great religions – there is 'no God but God'.

Unlike Jesus, Muhammad was a worldly person, a talented political leader. This has led Islam to believe that there is no such thing as a secular state; religion and politics are inseparable. The law in Islam is derived not from the holy book, the Koran, although according to Muslims it contains the word of God. Muslims follow the words and actions of Muhammad and his followers. These are known as the Sunnah and are collected in the *Hadith*. The Koran and the Sunnah are what constitute Islamic *Shariah* law, a system of social morality describing the way a person should live according to the will of God. Contravention of the *Shariah* is, therefore, not a breach of a law of a state; it is, rather, an offence against God himself.

The early achievements of Muhammad were astonishing. His religious conversion happened when he was forty years of age, when the Arabian Peninsula was little more than a group

CHRISTIANITY AND ISLAM

of small autonomous states based largely on tribal principles. Mostly nomadic, the people of these states tended to be animists who worshipped spirits associated with a particular place. There was no codified law and the only thing stopping crime was a fear of terrible vengeance. Although, when compared with the sophisticated civilisations of Byzantium and Persia, it seems fairly primitive, the region did have something that would stand it in good stead – the common language of Arabic. By the death of Muhammad, the new monotheistic faith had conquered Arabia and unified the diverse tribes of the Arabian Peninsula into a formidable force.

Muhammad was succeeded by four remarkable men – the Rashidun (Rightly Guided Ones) who also achieved great things on behalf of their faith. The Persians were dealt with and, within ten years of the Prophet's death, the Sassanid Persians had been defeated and forced to flee Mesopotamia. The Arabs next swept like a tidal wave through North Africa, capturing Syria and Egypt and crossed the Straits of Gibraltar into Europe, capturing a large part of the Iberian Peninsula. The Byzantine Empire was a more difficult nut to crack, however, and although the Arabs captured Cyprus, Rhodes and Cos and twice laid siege to Constantinople, they failed to conquer Anatolia.

Thirty years after Muhammad's death, in AD 656, Uthman (r. 644-656), the successor to the second caliph Omar (r. 634-644), was assassinated. He was originally succeeded by Ali (r. 656-661), the Prophet's first cousin and the man who had married his daughter, Fatima (605 or 615-633). However, the Arab General Muawiyah (r. 661-680), governor of Syria and a member of the Umayyads, a powerful Mecca family, was opposed to Ali becoming caliph. Islam's great division resulted from the defeat of Ali's candidature by the Umayyads. On one side were the Sunnis – 'people of the sunnah' – and on the other the Shia

– 'partisans' of Ali – who continue to believe the Umayyad claim to the caliphate was not legitimate. The split continues to this day with about 10 per cent of the world's Muslims being Shiite and located in Iran and India, and the remainder being Sunni. The split in the seventh century still resonates in the region's politics to this day.

The Umayyads made Damascus in Syria their capital but, in 750, they were defeated by the Abbasids. This rival revolutionary movement was based in Persia which meant that the centre of power shifted to the new city of Baghdad, founded in 762, thirty kilometres from Babylon. A golden age ensued in which Islam helped to create some of the greatest achievements of human history. The legacy of Greek philosophy was embraced and developed and taken back to Europe through Arab Spain. Notable caliphs in this cultural flowering were Harun al-Rashid (r. 786-809) and al-Ma'mun (r. 813-33). At the same time, Arabic began to replace existing languages. Greek was replaced in Syria, Palestine and Egypt and in the Arabian Peninsula Arabic replaced Aramaic, a once great language now spoken only in a few villages north of Damascus and in northern Iraq. The Coptic language in Egypt also began to disappear, although it survived until around the seventeenth century. The Persian language survived the arrival of Islam but Farsi adopted Arabic script and many Arabic words entered the language. Islam spread as far as Samarkand and all the way to India but languages survived, Arabic being the language only of religious observance. It is estimated that today only around a fifth of the world's Muslims speak Arabic.

It took until the tenth century for Turkey to convert to Islam but the Turkish language survived, although many Arabic words were incorporated into it, and they began to use Arabic script in writing their language. In the twelfth century, Persian became the literary language of western Asia and the Turkish language was greatly affected by that. Thus did the occupants of the Middle East come to speak just three main languages – Arabic, Persian and Turkish.

Three minorities resisted Islamisation and stayed true to their own national identities – the Kurds, the Berbers and the Armenians. The Armenians have had a continuous national identity since the sixth century BC, occupying parts of eastern Turkey and Transcaucasia. They claim to be the world's oldest Christian nation and were an independent state until the fourteenth century when they were absorbed into the Islamic Empire. Although dispersed now across the Middle East and around the world, they steadfastly retain their identity, religion and culture. The Kurds have never had their own state and today inhabit territory that runs in an arc from northwestern Iran through northeastern Iraq and Syria into eastern Turkey.

Of course, it is one thing to capture territories and quite another to govern them. To a large extent, as we have seen, the Arabs benefitted from the fact that the Byzantines and Persians were gravely weakened by their struggles against each other, but their rulers had also been very unpopular with the peoples over whom they ruled. In the beginning, the Arab warriors who conquered the Middle East numbered no more than a few hundred thousand. Those Muslims who marched with them who were not pure Arabs – Persians, Egyptians, Levantines or Berbers – were known as *mawalis* or 'clients'. But distinguishing a person by race is contrary to the teaching of the Koran and soon, with intermarriage with *mawali* women increasingly common, the old distinction began to vanish. In this way, the term 'Arab' moved away from its original meaning of a Bedouin nomad of the Arabian Peninsula to what it means today – a person who speaks Arabic and whose culture is Arabic. Thus did ethnic equality begin to prevail during the period that the Abbasids were in power.

Baghdad became the hub of a huge area of free trade, Arab ships plying the oceans and seas as far as China, Sumatra, India and Madagascar. There were astonishing advances in science, literature and the arts. As with many large empires, though, its decline was a direct result of its sheer size. Distant colonies could not be effectively governed. Egypt and eastern Persia were ruled by local military leaders who became autonomous and there were numerous examples of the weakness of the empire caused by religious sects and the seizure of power by the very soldiers who were supposed to protect the caliph and the empire. Around 877, Egypt and Syria were lost to a Turk named Ibn Tulun (r. 868-84) and these two nations would remain united – with just a few intervals – until the Ottomans took control of the entire region in the sixteenth century.

The Arab Islamic Empire now encompassed a great deal of the known world. In the early eighth century they not only held Spain but also half of France, although they soon withdrew from there. A new threat arose in 969 when Egypt was invaded from the west by troops of the Fatimid Dynasty, the name of which was derived from the daughter of the Prophet. Originating in Syria, the Fatimids were a Shiite movement dedicated to the overthrow of the Abbasids. They founded a rival caliphate to Baghdad and made Cairo their capital. Their empire was soon every bit as splendid as that of the Abbasids, stretching right across the Maghreb and the Mediterranean to Sicily. Oriental trade, upon which the Abbasid caliphate depended, was re-routed to the Red Sea from the Persian Gulf and Cairo flourished.

External Threats

In AD 330, Roman Emperor Constantine founded a city bearing his name on the site of Byzantium on the Bosphorus, naming it Constantinople (modern-day Istanbul). It took on the role of capital of the eastern part of the Roman Empire but was soon vying with its ancient twin for glory and splendour. When Emperor Theodosius (r. 379-392) died, the Roman Empire was split between his two sons but the western half of the empire based at Rome would soon collapse in the face of increasingly devastating barbarian invasions, while in the east, the Byzantine Empire was born. Byzantium retained control of Syria, Palestine, Egypt, the Balkans and Asia Minor and would hold on to the Middle East for a further three centuries. For two hundred years peace was maintained with the ambitious Sassanian Persians through diplomacy but when Byzantine Emperor Justinian 'the Great' decided to try to regain the provinces of the former western part of the empire the Persian danger became greatest. They persistently invaded and occupied Syria between 534 and 628 but were each time repulsed by Byzantine troops. Egypt and Asia Minor were captured in 616 and Constantinople was itself besieged by the Persian armies. Emperor Heraclius (r. 610-641) defeated the Persians and succeeded in restoring his empire's borders as they were before the Persian conquest, but the two states were inevitably weakened by the constant strife.

The Crusades

By the first half of the eleventh century, the three former superpowers, the Byzantine, Fatimid and Abbasid Empires, were all in serious decline. The scene was set for change and it emerged from central Asia when Oghuz Turkish nomads – the Seljuks – invaded Persia, capturing Baghdad in 1050. Syria and Palestine followed in 1071, forcing the Fatimids to retreat to Egypt. The Seljuks now sat at the centre of an empire that included Syria and Palestine, Mesopotamia and Persia. Next on the Seljuk agenda were the rich lands of the Byzantine Empire. Led by Sultan Alp Arslan (r. 1063-72), they inflicted a heavy defeat on a large Byzantine army at the Battle of Manzikert (1071), capturing the Byzantine Emperor Romanos IV Diogenes (r. 1068-71). The Byzantines lost all their territories in Asia Minor and the Seljuks settled in Anatolia.

Byzantium had acted as a buffer between Europe and the Arabs but with every prospect of the empire collapsing in the face of these new threats, Emperor Alexius Comnenus (r. 1081-1118) appealed directly to Pope Urban II for help. At the Council of Clermont in 1095, Urban exhorted Europeans to take up arms against the threat from the east and wrest the Holy Land from the Seljuks:

> '…this land which you inhabit, shut in on all sides by the seas and surrounded by the mountain peaks, is too narrow for your large population; nor does it abound in wealth; and it furnishes scarcely food enough for its cultivators. Hence it is that you murder one another, that you wage war, and that frequently you perish by mutual wounds. Let therefore hatred depart from among you, let your quarrels end, let wars cease, and let all dissensions and controversies slumber. Enter upon the road

to the Holy Sepulchre; wrest that land from the wicked race, and subject it to yourselves... God has conferred upon you above all nations great glory in arms. Accordingly undertake this journey for the remission of your sins, with the assurance of the imperishable glory of the Kingdom of Heaven.'

The Crusades were born and the first was initially a success. Jerusalem was taken in 1099 and the Crusaders massacred its Jewish and Muslim inhabitants. Four new Crusader states were established in the region they named 'Outremer' (Over the Sea) – the County of Edessa, the Principality of Antioch, the County of Tripoli and the Kingdom of Jerusalem. Godfrey of Bouillon (1060-1100), the Duke of Lower Lorraine, became the first ruler of the new kingdom, although he refused the title of 'king', contending that the only King of Jerusalem was Jesus Christ. Jerusalem was fairly peripheral to the Seljuks and the Fatimids and the Crusader states were not seen as a threat to Islam. Therefore, after one failed attempt by the Fatimids to recapture the city, the Crusaders were largely left to their own devices.

After the fall of Edessa to the Turks in 1144, a Second Crusade (1145-47) was launched. One part of this initiative was to try to displace the Moors in the Iberian Peninsula. Lisbon was recaptured as well as other territories. In the east, the Crusaders unaccountably ignored the plight of Edessa and made for Jerusalem where there was actually no real threat at the time. Some 50,000 Crusaders also launched an unsuccessful attack on the friendly city of Damascus. The victor at Damascus, Nur ad-Din, King of Mosul (r. 1146-74) went on to conquer Syria and, in 1149, he defeated Raymond, Prince of Antioch (1115-49), one of the principal Christian leaders in Outremer.

In 1187, led by Saladin (r. 1174-93), a Kurdish military commander of genius, the Muslim states were joined in a *jihad* (holy war) against the Crusaders in Jerusalem. Saladin routed the Crusaders at the Battle of Hattin, recapturing Jerusalem but, unlike his Crusader predecessors almost a hundred years earlier, he showed mercy to those who surrendered.

A Third Crusade was launched in 1189 that lasted until 1192. The instigators were two erstwhile enemies, Henry II of England (r. 1154-89) and Philip II of France (r. 1180-1223). When Henry died, his successor, Richard I 'the Lionheart' (r. 1189-99) took his place and the large army of the Holy Roman Emperor, Frederick I 'Barbarossa' (r. 1155-90), was added to this force. The elderly Frederick drowned in a river in southeastern Anatolia while en route to the Holy Land.

There were some early successes and Acre was captured but there were disagreements about the division of the spoils. The lack of trust persuaded King Philip and Leopold V of Austria (r. 1177-94) to return home. Meanwhile, at the Battle of Arsuf, Richard defeated Saladin but lacked sufficient forces to retake Jerusalem. He agreed a truce with the Arab general and set out for England in October 1192. On his journey home, he was captured by Leopold of Austria and handed over to the Holy Roman Emperor, Henry VI (r. 1191-97). A ransom was paid in 1194 and he was released.

When Pope Innocent III (Pope 1198-1216) urged a Fourth Crusade, European leaders had little stomach for it but the Italian Count Boniface of Montferrat (1150-1207) set off at the head of a force. His army made it only as far as Constantinople which they destroyed after Emperor Alexius IV Angelus (r. 1203-04) reneged on promises of rich pickings if they helped him depose his uncle Emperor Alexius III Angelus (r. 1195-1203). The Crusaders founded a Latin Empire there, installing Baldwin of Flanders (r. 1204-05) on its throne. This entity would remain in place until 1261. Meanwhile, the Holy Land was forgotten.

EXTERNAL THREATS

There were another four Crusades – in 1216, 1228, 1248 and 1270 – all of which ended in failure. By the end of the thirteenth century, the Mamlukes of Egypt were rulers of the Muslim world. They recaptured Acre in 1291, marking the end of the Crusades.

The Mongols

With the expulsion of the Crusaders, Islam now had the Middle East to itself. In Egypt, Saladin's Ayyubid dynasty lasted only from 1171 to 1260, replaced by the Mamlukes, mainly of Kipchak and Turkic origin, who, following the death of Saladin, became increasingly involved in the internal court politics of the country. The Mamluke dynasty was founded in 1250 and, at the end of the thirteenth century, they incorporated Syria into their empire. Meanwhile, the Seljuks took advantage of the decline of Byzantium by increasing their territory in Anatolia. Their dynasty in Asia Minor became known as 'the Sultanate of Rûm' – 'Rûm' being Persian for Rome. At its height, this Muslim inheritor of much of Rome's Eastern Empire stretched right across Anatolia, from Antalya on the Mediterranean coast to the town of Sinop on the Black Sea. To the far east of what is modern-day Turkey, it reached as far as Lake Van and its western extent was near to the town of Denizli, not far from the Aegean. They encouraged trade with caravanserais carrying goods from Iran and Central Asia to the ports and they formed a strong trading relationship with the Genoese. The wealth engendered by such activities helped the sultanate to incorporate other small Turkish states that had been established after the Battle of Manzikert.

In the mid-thirteenth century, however, with the sultanate weakened by uprisings, a new threat appeared on the eastern horizon – the Mongols who emerged from central Asia intent on capturing the fertile lands of the Fertile Crescent. In 1220, Genghis Khan (r. 1206-27) conquered Persia and in 1243 the Seljuks were defeated at the Battle of Köse Dag by Bayju (*fl.* 1230-60). After the Sultan fled the battle, the Seljuks were forced to swear allegiance to the Mongols and became their vassals. Then, in 1258, Hulagu (r. 1256-65), the grandson of Genghis, seized Baghdad, wiping away the last vestiges of the Abbasid caliphate.

Egypt and Syria were next in the path of what appeared to be an unstoppable force. The Mamlukes rose to the occasion, however, defeating the Mongols in 1260 at the Battle of Ain Jalut in Palestine. It was the first time that the Mongols had been permanently beaten in direct combat on a battlefield and it was one of the most important battles ever fought, saving the Muslim world from being completely overrun. However, to the disappointment of Christians in the West who had harboured hopes that he would accept their faith, the Mongol khan announced in 1295 that he had converted to Islam.

A Weakened Middle East

The Crusaders left little of lasting value in the Middle East, apart from a few castles. If anything, their legacy was a weakening of the superior civilisation they had encountered. One commentator has noted:

'Although the epoch of the Crusades ignited a genuine economic and cultural revolution in Western Europe, in the Orient these holy wars led to long centuries of decadence and obscurantism. Assaulted from all quarters, the Muslim world turned in on itself. It became over-sensitive, defensive, intolerant, and sterile – attitudes that grew steadily worse as

world-wide evolution continued. Henceforth progress was the embodiment of "the other". Modernism became alien.'
Amin Maalouf, *The Crusades Through Arab Eyes*,
London, Saqi Books, 1984

The Muslim civilisation that the Crusaders fought was far more sophisticated in many ways, and it is often remarked how backward, for instance, the Muslims thought the West to be in medical practice. In one way, however, they were themselves backward – in the creation of lasting political institutions. In Europe, feudal society was developing and although it was far from perfect, especially for the peasant or serf class, at least there were rights and obligations for every level of society that were more often than not respected. In the Muslim world, the tribal democracies, governed by a council that limited the powers of the ruler, had gradually been replaced by despotism. This was compounded by the fact that the Mamlukes refused to countenance any kind of hereditary system and their rulers, therefore, were not on the throne for long, more often than not deposed by a stronger rival.

The Mongol Empire was by this time in decline and no longer posed a threat to the Middle East. A new one was emerging, however, from the direction of Asia Minor.

The Middle East to 1800

The Ottoman Empire: Origins and Early Rulers

The former territories of the Byzantines in Asia Minor were now in the hands of a dozen or so fairly independent Turkish ghazis or warrior chieftains. One of these was Osman (r. 1280-99 and 1299-1326). According to one version of events, Osman's father Ertugrul (r. 1230-81) led his Kayi tribe west out of Central Asia into Anatolia to escape the advancing Mongols. Having pledged allegiance to the Sultanate of Rûm, he was allowed to establish a *beylik*, or principality. He expanded his territory, capturing the Byzantine town of Thebasion whose name he changed to Sogut. It became his capital and it was there that Osman was born in 1258.

Osman became *Bey*, or chief, in 1280 when his father died and by then mercenaries were flooding into his realm from across the Muslim world, hoping to share in some of the rich pickings to be enjoyed as the Byzantine Empire declined. Refugees were also pouring in, fleeing from the Mongols. Osman moulded the mercenaries into a formidable fighting force and began to expand his territory still more at the expense of the Byzantines. At the same time, however, he ensured that he did not raise the ire of the more powerful Turkish states that neighboured his own. Osman died in Bursa in 1326, having founded an empire that would govern across three continents for the next six hundred years.

SHIFTING SANDS

The early rulers of the Ottoman Empire were statesmanlike, chivalrous and tolerant towards the Christians under their control. This was especially true after Osman's grandson Murad I (r. 1362-89) led his army across the Hellespont that separated Asia Minor from Europe and extended the Ottoman Empire into the Christian Balkan states. Murad encouraged all non-Muslims in his empire to become citizens and everyone, regardless of ethnicity or religion, had the opportunity to rise to the highest offices of empire. He was assassinated after the Battle of Kosovo in 1389 in which his army defeated the Serbs but his legacy was a great empire with many of the institutions established for which the Ottoman Empire would become known. He introduced the title of sultan (an Arabic word meaning 'strength', 'authority', or 'rulership') in 1383 and created the corps of Janissaries – elite infantry units that formed the sultan's household troops and guards. He devised the Devşirme recruiting system, an annual practice of kidnapping Christian boys from Balkan villages, converting them to Islam and training them for military or civil service in the Empire, most notably as Janissaries. He created the two provinces of his empire – Anadolu (Anatolia) and Rumelia (Europe, meaning the Balkans).

Murad's son Bayezid (r. 1389-1403) conquered much of the rest of Anatolia by 1390 and, between 1389 and 1395, took the areas of modern Bulgaria and Greece. Only defeat by the Wallachians at the fierce Battle of Rovine prevented him from advancing beyond the Danube. In 1394, he laid siege to Constantinople, still capital of the Byzantine Empire, and two years later, at the Battle of Nicopolis, he defeated a coalition of Christian forces led by King Sigismund of Hungary (r. 1387-1437). Constantinople was besieged until 1402 but there was relief when Bayezid found himself facing a new threat from the east – the armies of the Central Asian warlord Timur (r. 1370-1405). The fearsome

THE MIDDLE EAST TO 1800

Timur had captured the Delhi Sultanate in 1398 and, as Bayezid began to annex the territory of Turkmen and Muslim rulers in Anatolia, Timur responded, claiming sovereignty over the Turkmen rulers who gratefully accepted his support. In 1400, he invaded Christian Armenia and Georgia before turning his attention to Syria, sacking Aleppo and Damascus and massacring their populations. Baghdad was captured in 1401 and 20,000 of its inhabitants were slaughtered. Moving on to Anatolia, Timur's army defeated Bayezid at the Battle of Ankara in July 1402 in which Bayezid was taken prisoner. Following his death in captivity, the Ottoman throne remained vacant for twelve years, during which time Bayezid's sons fought a civil war. In 1413, Mehmed I (r. 1413-21) emerged triumphant. Meanwhile, Timur, who had come very close to bringing an end to the fledgling Ottoman Empire, died in 1405 on his way to launch an invasion of Ming Dynasty China.

With Timur out of the way, the Ottoman Empire revived, producing in the mid-fifteenth century one of its greatest sultans – Mehmed II 'the Conqueror' (r. 1444-46, 1451-81). Mehmed achieved one of the great ambitions of Islamic tradition – the conquest of Constantinople. In April 1453, he laid siege to the city with a massive army of up to 200,000 troops and a navy of 320 ships. Fifty-seven days later, the city fell and Mehmed moved his capital there from Adrianople. He captured Serbia, in 1459, Morea in the southern Balkans in 1460, and the Empire of Trebizond in the northeastern corner of Anatolia in 1461. Wallachia followed in 1462 and Bosnia a year later. The Crimean Khanate was invaded in 1475 and Albania fell in 1478. There was nothing left of the Byzantine Empire.

Mehmed's troops terrified Europeans, reaching the outskirts of Venice in 1478 and invading Italy in 1480 but his death in 1483 probably saved the West from further incursions. For the next two hundred years the Turks were the bogeymen of Europe and, indeed, in 1529 and 1683, they came close to capturing Vienna and defeating the Hapsburg Empire.

The empire continued to flourish economically due to its control of the trade routes between Europe and Asia but a succession of good rulers also helped to expand its borders. Sultan Selim I (r. 1512-20) focused on Asia, winning the Battle of Chaldiran against Shah Ismail of Safavid Persia in 1514, and also succeeding in occupying Syria and Palestine and capturing Egypt. The ruler of Mecca offered Selim the keys to Islam's Holy City and named him 'Protector of the Holy Places' and the Prophet's standard and cloak were transported to Constantinople. The empire reached its greatest extent under Suleiman the Magnificent (r. 1520-66) who took Belgrade in 1521 and captured southern and central parts of the Kingdom of Hungary. He unsuccessfully laid siege to Vienna in 1529 and captured Baghdad from Persian control in 1535, giving the empire control of Mesopotamia and providing his navy with access to the Persian Gulf. In 1537, North Africa as far as Morocco came into the empire. In 1555, the Caucasus was partitioned between the Safavids and Ottomans and it would remain thus until the eighteenth century. Under Suleiman, the Ottoman Empire also expanded into Somalia and the Horn of Africa. By his death, the population of the empire had increased to around fifteen million people and stretched across three continents. Of the Arabic-speaking world, only Morocco in the west of North Africa and the southeast and central Arabian Peninsula remained outside the empire. Meanwhile, its navy controlled the Mediterranean and its culture flourished, the great architect Sinan helping to make Istanbul/Constantinople one of the world's great cities.

The Ottoman Empire lasted five hundred years but its decline began about halfway through that period. By the end of the seventeenth century, it was a pale imitation of the empire that had so terrified Europe in the fifteenth and sixteenth centuries. There were a number of reasons for the gradual decline that would continue until 1827 – bad advisers and senior officials, ill-equipped armies and corruption – but the principal cause was the weakness of the thirteen sultans who ruled from 1566 until 1703. Weakness at the centre allowed provincial elites to emerge who paid little heed to what the sultan wanted. In Europe, armies and weaponry became increasingly sophisticated while little changed in the way Ottoman troops were trained and equipped, and the Janissaries, in particular, resisted change. Constant warfare damaged the imperial finances, causing inflation, and revenues fell as Europe increasingly looked westwards and exploited new maritime trade routes at the expense of the old overland routes the Ottomans controlled. Following Vasco da Gama's voyage around the Cape of Good Hope in 1497, opening a new route to India and the Far East, the old route through Egypt and the Red Sea lost a great deal of its traffic. When bullion flooded Europe from Spanish possessions in the New World, the result was the depreciation of the Ottoman silver currency, high inflation in the empire and still higher taxes.

Ottoman society was heavily centralised, almost all of the land being owned by the state. The best land was divided amongst the military aristocracy but the system was never allowed to become hereditary. Hence, although it was feudal, it was a very different type of feudalism from the European version that was a necessary stage in the move towards capitalism. Therefore, the Ottomans fell behind in terms of industrial power and material wealth. It has to be said also that the sultanate itself brought huge problems. The wellbeing of the empire depended entirely on the sultan and when, as was often the case, he was incompetent or ineffective, the empire suffered. There was never any chance of the sultan sharing power and the barbaric practice of imperial fratricide – older brother eliminating other brothers who might be rivals for the throne – created an atmosphere of fear and distrust in the royal palace, mothers intriguing against others to try to keep their sons alive. The heir apparent was often locked up in a small room known as 'the cage' to keep him from harm. This practice led to physically weak or even deformed sultans who had suffered from years of incarceration.

Finally, when Grand Vizier Kara Mustafa Pasha's (1634/5-83) huge army was defeated at the gates of Vienna in 1683 by allied Hapsburg, German and Polish forces, the expansionist ambitions of the Ottomans were at an end, although European fears of a Muslim advance did not fade from public consciousness for years. The Ottoman Empire began to become financially beholden to European powers, and lost territory. By about 1853, Tsar Nicholas I of Russia (r. 1825-55) could describe it as the 'sick man of Europe'.

Russia was long the scourge of the Ottoman Empire. For two hundred years they sparred with each other, periods of hostilities interrupted by times of uneasy peace. Parts of the empire, such as the Grecian Morea and Belgrade, were lost and, under the humiliating 1774 Treaty of Küchük Kainarji that ended the Russo-Turkish War of 1768-74, the Crimea was declared independent and Russia was given the right to protect Christians in the Ottoman Empire.

Safavid Persia (1501-1736)

Following the death of Timur and the decline of the empire he had created, there was a political vacuum in Persia. Religious communities began to emerge as political entities, the most powerful of which was the Safavid Qizilbash. One of its leaders was the man who would found the Safavid Dynasty — Shah Ismail I (r. 1501-24). After various conquests, Ismail proclaimed himself Shahanshah of Iran and declared that Shi'ism was the official religion of his kingdom. Within ten years he had established complete control over all of Persia. Having dealt with problems caused by Uzbeks on his eastern borders, he was now faced with the hostility of the Ottomans who objected to the Safavid recruitment of some of the Turkmen tribes of Anatolia. In 1511, there was a pro-Shia and pro-Safavid uprising in the Ottoman Empire that led Bayezid to send an army through Anatolia to the plain of Chaldiran, where Ismail's much smaller and less well-equipped army was defeated. The Safavid capital, Tabriz, was captured and Ismail was taken prisoner. The empire survived this catastrophe although the war carried on. After Ismail's death the old tribal rivalries erupted again and between 1524 and 1533 there was civil war. Finally, Ismail's son, Shah Tahmasp I (r. 1524-76) regained control.

The Uzbeks continued to be a problem on the Safavid Empire's eastern frontier and during Tahmasp's reign they invaded the eastern provinces five times while the Ottomans invaded four times in the West. When the Safavids defeated the Uzbeks at Herat in 1528, it was partly as a result of the firearms they had been acquiring since the great defeat at Chaldiran against better-equipped Ottoman troops. However, Tahmasp still doubted his troops' ability to defeat the Ottomans, preferring to cede territory rather than directly engage with them. Campaigns by the Ottomans in 1534 and 1548-49 forced the shah to move his court to Qazvin and, in 1553, after the Ottomans destroyed a number of royal palaces, Tahmasp was obliged to sign a treaty with his enemy which at least ensured peace for the next twenty years and gave Ottoman recognition to the Safavid Empire. The Ottomans returned various captured towns but retained eastern

Anatolia and Mesopotamia. Humiliating though the terms of the treaty were, they allowed the Safavid Empire to continue to exist.

Tahmasp was succeeded by his son Ismail II (r. 1576-77) whose reign was short-lived and filled with horrific bloodletting of his family members and others. He also turned against the Shia religion, probably because of his hatred for his pious father, and tried to introduce Sunni orthodoxy. After just fourteen months on the throne he was poisoned by his Circassian half-sister.

Mohammad Khodabanda (r. 1578-87) succeeded him and ruled for ten years, filled with palace intrigue and murder. Meanwhile, when rebellion, led by his son Abbas (r. 1588-1629), broke out in Khorasan, Persia's enemies took advantage and attacked. The Uzbeks were repulsed in 1578 and the Ottomans invaded the Persian territories of Georgia and Shirvan, Transcaucasia, Dagestan, Kurdistan and Luristan. Eventually, with the Ottomans deep in Persian territory and the Uzbeks encroaching in the north, Shah Mohammad handed power to Abbas who, over the next ten years, restored central authority to the empire and reorganised the government. He immediately concluded an agreement with the Ottomans, allowing them to retain their territorial gains and succeeded in reducing the importance of tribal loyalties, increasing his own and the empire's security. He moved the capital to Isfahan, building a new city next to the ancient Persian one and destroyed the power of the militant group, the Qizilbash, effectively creating a new national Persian monarchy with its own distinctive identity. He also recovered territory from the Uzbeks and forced the Portuguese out of Bahrain in 1602 and Hormuz in 1622.

After Abbas died with no heir — he had had his last capable son killed because he was suspicious of him — the Safavid Empire went into decline. New rivals such as Russian Muscovy arose and the European trading companies used their superior navies to take control of western Indian Ocean trade routes. Persia found itself cut off from lucrative markets although its overland trade with Central and North Europe flourished in the second half of the seventeenth century. The Dutch and the English deprived the empire of its precious metal supplies and Safavid shahs after Abbas were rendered ineffectual, although they still enjoyed lavish lifestyles. In 1722, an Afghan force captured Isfahan and deposed Shah Sultan Husayn (r. 1694-1722). The Afghan leader Mahmud Hotak I (r. 1717-25) was acknowledged as the new ruler. After the assassination of the Persian military genius, Nader Shah (r. 1736-47), who had regained the empire and had begun to expand it again, a brief puppet regime ruled, purely in order to give legitimacy to a new dynasty from central Iran – the Zand dynasty. Its leader Karim Khan (r. 1751-79) eventually felt strong enough to take control and the Safavid era was at an end.

The Ottoman Empire After 1800

Foreign Influence

As the eighteenth century ended, the caliph – as the sultan was now calling himself, re-introducing a title 'Caliph of Islam', unused for five hundred years – retained full authority over Sunni Islam. Admittedly, the Arab-speaking provinces of the empire were largely autonomous, ruled by their own local dynasties such as the Druze emirs in Mount Lebanon or the Mamlukes who governed Egypt and Mesopotamia. The caliphate began to assume spiritual authority over all Muslims, even those who were not ruled by Muslims.

The days of the Crusades and foreign incursions into Islamic territory were long gone, but the major powers were now far subtler in the way that they infiltrated the Middle East. In order to help the economy of the Ottoman Empire, a series of immunities and privileges – known as Capitulations – was given to foreigners. These contracts were bilateral acts, beneficial to each side, that were signed by successive caliphs and the Christian nations. The first of these arrangements was given as early as 1453 to the Genoese in Constantinople's Galata suburb shortly after the Ottomans had captured the city from the Byzantines. Francis I of France (r. 1515-47) was granted Capitulations in 1535 after he had supported the Ottomans against the Habsburgs. They covered a range of matters and were not merely commercial devices. The French, for example, were granted full religious liberty within the Ottoman Empire as well as the right of guarding the empire's Christian holy places. Non-Muslim foreigners living in the Ottoman Empire were not subject to the law of the empire, no matter how serious the crime with which they had been charged. They were dealt with, rather, by special consular courts. Russia, too, enjoyed the right of protection of Orthodox Christians within the empire.

The Ottomans were not alone in issuing concessions to foreigners. Shah Abbas I of Persia forged relationships with the English and the Dutch East India Companies, issuing them with special privileges. The English East India Company helped him to oust the Portuguese from Hormuz in 1622 and in return was given concessions in the port of Bandar Abbas. Later rulers followed his example but were, in reality, giving away a part of the economy of the Safavid Empire.

Unlike during the Golden Age of the first Islamic Empire, the Muslims of the time expressed little interest in the culture and crafts of foreigners. Foreigners had been employed as officials in government but now they were generally Turkish who had little skill or wish to learn about the outside world. The foreigners' knowledge and skills had been welcomed but now there was little curiosity about why the Western Christian powers suddenly seemed to be so far ahead of Islamic society. Only in military and naval matters was there any interest and these helped to encourage development in the associated fields of mathematics, navigation and cartography. Printing had revolutionised Europe and the new technology was introduced in the late fifteenth century by the Jews, Armenians and Greeks, but in the Ottoman Empire printing in Arabic or Turkish was prohibited by religious leaders. Therefore, the Renaissance and the Reformation and Counter-Reformation, with all the great ideas they engendered, passed largely unnoticed in the Islamic world.

The Reforming Selim III

Although the empire continued to be accepted across the Middle East, even in areas where there was a degree of autonomy, the French Revolution began to change things. Revolutionary ideas started to drift eastwards. Sultan Selim III (r. 1789-1807) was a calligrapher, a musician and a poet, a very modern man who would become a reformist ruler. When he assumed the throne, the empire was at war with Austria and Russia, a conflict that lasted from 1787 to 1792 and his reforms were put on hold until that was over. To begin with, he reformed the Ottoman army, bringing in European officers and military experts to provide training and he purchased modern weapons and built armament factories. The navy was modernised and a navigation school was opened. There was hostility to the changes and Selim was forced to limit the size of his new, modern force to 10,000 men. He also introduced reforms in government, especially in the area of finance, and extended the availability of education. Naval engineering, military engineering, medical and military science colleges were opened and a plan for state education was introduced. Special privileges such as fiefs, granted to the military elite, were abolished and the empire began to look beyond its borders, opening embassies in Britain, France, Prussia and Austria. Selim's changes did not reach his Arab provinces, however, where local rulers enjoyed a great deal of autonomy. The al-Azm family controlled Damascus for most of the eighteenth century; Sidon, on the Syrian coast, was ruled by a Bosnian, Ahmad al-Jazzar (1708 or 1720-1804). In Egypt whose rich farmland provided the empire with coffee, wheat and rice, there was an eternal power-struggle between the Ottomans and the Mamlukes.

Egypt was a vital part of the empire, guarding the main route to India and the East and in 1798 it became another theatre in the war between the great European rivals, Britain and France. Napoleon Bonaparte, head of the French army, had planned to invade Britain, but, having concluded that his navy was not strong enough to take on the Royal Navy, opted instead to block Britain's access to its lucrative trade interests in India by launching a military expedition aimed at capturing Egypt from the Ottomans. Once he had achieved this, he intended to 'establish relations with the Indian princes and, together with them, attack the English in their possessions'. In short, his aim was to destroy Britain's empire.

Bonaparte landed near Alexandria in July 1798, marched his force up the Nile and defeated the Mamluke army at the Battle of the Pyramids. He lost 300 men, but around 6,000 Egyptian troops died. Entering Cairo, he established a military government, the two Ottoman-appointed beys having fled. He cleverly demonstrated respect for Islam and even claimed that he and his troops were under the special protection of the Prophet, having come, he told local officials, to free them from Mamluke tyranny. He established a form of indirect rule, appointing local political leaders to *diwans* – councils – that were chaired by a French officer but he failed to win over the Egyptians who were dismayed to see the promotion of Christian Copts to senior positions as tax collectors and civil servants, and Christians being recruited into the Egyptian army.

Napoleon's dream of following in the illustrious footsteps of Alexander the Great was not to be. Sultan Selim allied his empire with Britain and Russia and in the Bay of Abukir on 1 August 1798, a British fleet under the command of Admiral

Horatio Nelson (1758-1805) destroyed a French fleet. The British now controlled the Mediterranean, rendering it impossible for Napoleon to strengthen his position because he was cut off from France. There was a further calamity when he advanced into Syria in an effort to stop Ottoman troops dispatched by the sultan. Finally, at Acre, Bonaparte was forced to retreat after he had laid siege to the city. With his campaign failing and growing political turmoil at home, he decided to return to France with a handful of followers. The French force that remained in Egypt under General Jean Baptiste Kléber (1753-1800) gamely held on for the next two years, quelling uprisings in Cairo and attacks by Ottoman troops supported by the British. Finally, they evacuated the country and returned to France.

It was but a brief interlude in the long history of Egypt, but it had a lasting impact. Firstly, it generated interest in the West in the Ottoman Empire and the Islamic world. It also marked the beginning of a tussle for control and influence in the Middle East amongst the superpowers. Initially, it was Britain and France who showed an interest but Russia soon joined in. Later in the new century, Germany and Italy would also take an interest in the region.

Egypt 1805-1848: the Rule of Muhammad Ali

By the late eighteenth century, the Ottoman Empire was so preoccupied with wars against European powers and rebellions by local chiefs that Egypt was able to operate with a degree of autonomy. The Mamluke beys who governed, however, were oppressive and unpopular. It was a strange system of government, a system of networked families working in tandem with merchants, guildspeople and religious leaders rather than a strong, centralised government. There was frequent internecine strife amongst the various Mamluke factions who vied for power but a remarkable individual would soon emerge to unify the country and carry out major reforms that would transform Egypt.

France's unpopular three-year occupation of Egypt ended in 1801 when a British-Ottoman expedition arranged for the French troops to be evacuated. An ethnic Albanian named Muhammad Ali (r. 1805-48) who had been born in what is now Greek Macedonia arrived in Egypt as second-in-command of an Albanian force that was part of the expedition. He worked cleverly to get the people of Egypt on his side in the struggle with the Mamlukes to fill the power vacuum left by the French and, in 1805, a group of prominent Egyptians helped him to seize power and take the role of Viceroy. The Mamlukes remained a threat, but Ali ruthlessly eliminated the problem, inviting around seventy-four Mamluke leaders to an event at the Cairo Citadel where they were killed.

Muhammad Ali ruled for the next forty years and during that time he re-invented Egypt. He aimed to create a state in imitation of the strong European powers, remodelling the country's bureaucracy and centralising it. He nationalised all land, raising taxes on it in order to provide a revenue stream for the country, and instituted what was effectively a monopoly in the country whereby all producers were forced to sell their products to the state. The state then resold these products both within the country and abroad. Farmers' incomes increased by large amounts. He believed that, if Egypt were to gain independence from the Ottoman Empire, it needed a powerful army and navy. His initial focus, therefore, was on reshaping the military along European lines. To do this, however, he first needed to build an industrial base. Factories were built in Cairo to produce weapons such as cannons and muskets and a shipyard was built at Alexandria to provide vessels for the Egyptian navy.

THE OTTOMAN EMPIRE AFTER 1800

Ultimately, the industrialisation of Egypt was rushed and many of the factories closed down in the 1840s when he was forced by the 1841 Treaty of London to reduce his army to just 18,000 men. But the new industrial focus extended beyond the military. He also established a textile industry that was intended to compete with European textile manufacturers. Ultimately, he did not achieve that, but at least tens of thousands of Egyptians found employment in the factories that were built.

All of this was not without difficulties for the ordinary Egyptian, however, and the *corvée* labour system he introduced — unpaid work on public projects — was intensely unpopular, people fleeing their villages to escape work in a factory or conscription into the army where conditions were harsh. He introduced conscription registers and a national census both to ensure he could effectively conscript from the population and also to make certain that taxes were paid. Men were sent to Europe to study both in order to be able to learn from European armies but also to become fluent in French so that they could translate military manuals into Arabic. Experts were brought in from Europe to provide training and hospitals and schools and colleges were built. A government printing press was launched and the first Arab-language newspaper, *al-Waqai'i al-Misriyyah*, was published. Muhammad Ali created a central, professional bureaucracy and divided Egypt into ten provinces that were individually responsible for tax collection and for maintaining law and order, but he retained all central authority in his own person, with family members, including his sons, occupying important government functions and loyal supporters being given grants of land. To fill the ranks of his growing army, Muhammad Ali looked to Sudan, invading in 1820 and annexing the northern part of the country, although he failed to bolster his army very much with Sudanese soldiers and still had to resort to conscripting Egyptians.

He introduced and experimented with new crops, the best of which turned out to be a strain of long-staple cotton known as Jumel that was particularly prized by the European textile industry and soon became Egypt's most lucrative cash crop. Irrigation was improved, canals were dredged and dams built so that the Nile flood could be stored and used in the summer when the river was low. This was all achieved using *corvée* labour, so many *fellahin* being put to work that the countryside became depopulated.

Muhammad Ali not only sought to transform Egypt, he also hoped to establish a hereditary dynasty for his family. It has been noted that he had no love for his Egyptian subjects and he favoured Turks or Circassians over Egyptians in his military and bureaucratic elite.

Egyptian Expansion

The 130,000-strong Egyptian army was soon in action. In 1811, it moved against the fundamentalist Wahhabis who had seized Medina and Mecca. The Wahhabi movement had been started by Muhammad ibn Abd al-Wahhab (1703-92) who had launched a Sunni Islam revivalist movement. Led by Muhammad Ali's son, Ibrahim (r. 1848), the Egyptians defeated the Wahhabis and captured the two holy cities, establishing an Egyptian presence in the Hijaz region of present-day Saudi Arabia. In 1820, as we have seen, parts of Sudan were added to Egypt and, in 1821, Ibrahim helped the Ottoman Empire to subdue rebellion in Greece and to recapture Athens. In return, Muhammad Ali was to become governor of the Peloponnese peninsula, but the Greek revolt soon became a *cause célèbre* in Europe and Ali was forced to leave Greece to the Ottomans. The Egyptian leader had wasted precious money and resources for nothing which persuaded him that henceforth he would campaign only on his own behalf. Therefore, in autumn 1831, he launched an invasion of Syria in search of raw materials, especially timber for shipbuilding. Ibrahim led his army through Lebanon and Syria and onwards into Anatolia where he won a victory over the Ottomans. His army was just one hundred and fifty miles from the Ottoman capital. Sultan Mahmud II (r. 1808-39) quickly conjured up the Treaty of Unkiar Skelessi by which Russia would help to defend the empire but the idea of Russian interference in the Ottoman Empire was anathema to Britain and France. Their diplomats rapidly persuaded the Ottomans and Muhammad Ali to conclude a treaty. The Egyptians did make some gains as Ibrahim was recognised in the treaty as governor of the Anatolian region of Adana and Greater Syria.

Britain was becoming concerned about Egypt's growing military and commercial power and an expeditionary force of British and Ottoman troops was sent to Beirut in Lebanon in 1840. Already hostile to Ibrahim's administration, the locals rose up against him, forcing him to flee back to Egypt. The result was the 1841 Treaty of London which forced Muhammad Ali to withdraw from all the territories he had conquered, apart from the Sudan, and to reduce his armed forces to 18,000 men. The Egyptian leader's dynastic ambitions were more than satisfied, however, because the treaty also stipulated that the governorship of Egypt should from that date on be a hereditary office held by his family. His descendants would rule Egypt for the next one hundred and eleven years, until the coup of 1952.

Still worried about Russian involvement with the Ottoman Empire, Britain took advantage of the tension between Egypt and the Ottomans to negotiate the Treaty of Balta Liman 1838 with the sultan. By this trade agreement, all monopolies within the Ottoman Empire were abolished and foreign goods were allocated the favourable tariff of 3 per cent. Coupled with rigorous application of the Capitulations by the major European powers, this agreement effectively ended Egypt's military power, its industrial development and its economic autonomy. Colleges and schools shut down, factories were abandoned and the ambitious public works initiatives ended. Furthermore, the West now enjoyed a greater involvement in the affairs of the Middle East, especially in those of Egypt.

All was not lost, however. With his centralised bureaucracy, Muhammad Ali had laid the foundation for a modern Egyptian state and his education system permitted greater social mobility than Egyptians could previously have dreamed of.

Sultan Mahmud II's Reforms

The man in charge of the Ottoman Empire while Muhammad Ali was re-inventing Egypt was Mahmud II. During Mahmud's reign, he endured territorial losses and was overshadowed by Muhammad Ali. He was also faced with the united power of the Janissaries, the *ulama* – the religious elite – and the *derebeys*, the feudal lords. Nonetheless, he achieved a great deal and was one of the most effective of the Ottoman Empire's late sultans. Mahmud perceived that his empire was being held back by stultifying political forces in his government. To achieve what he wanted, however, he had to move cautiously against a backdrop of unrest amongst the European citizens of his empire.

He began his reign by pacifying the provinces and bringing them under central control once again before turning to his internal problems. He first dealt with the feudal lords, bribing the Janissaries to help him. Then on 15 June 1826, when the Janissaries rebelled against proposed military reforms, he massacred them, wiping away the military unit that had helped to establish and maintain Ottoman power. He was now free to

THE OTTOMAN EMPIRE AFTER 1800

push through his reforms, beginning with an army modelled on those of the European powers, a force he named 'the triumphant soldiers of Muhammad'. British, French and Prussian officers were brought in to train the troops and in 1827 he also founded a medical school for the military in Istanbul. The Imperial War College opened in 1834, based on the French training academy, the Ecole Spéciale Militaire de Saint-Cyr. As had happened in Egypt, students were sent abroad to study.

Mahmud also launched a reorganisation of government bureaucracy, creating ministries in imitation of those in European administrations and increasing the wages of his officials in an attempt to eliminate corruption. The turban and the robe were replaced by the fez and the frock coat and there was better training for officials who were taught in French. The first newspaper in Ottoman-Turkish, *Takvim-i Vekayi*, began publication in 1831 to keep his civil servants informed about what was happening in government. Mahmud also reopened embassies in European capitals and an emphasis was placed on providing translation services and teaching European languages to Ottoman officials.

There remained the issue of the *ulama*, the religious elite. It was the leading *ulama*, the Shayk al-Islam, who had turned against the reforms of Sultan Selim III and had him replaced with Mustafa IV (r. 1807-08). Mahmud determined, therefore, to limit the power of these religious leaders. Until then, they had been independent of the state, but Mahmud cleverly incorporated the office of the Shayk al-Islam into the state bureaucracy. He also took steps to divert the revenue from which the religious authorities benefitted into a new entity known as the Ministry of Religious Endowments. With these measures he removed a great deal of the power of the religious establishment.

Tanzimat (1839-76)

The new elite Mahmud created, nicknamed 'the French knowers', were given the best positions in the army and civil service and zealously continued his reforms long after his death. The period from 1839 to 1876 is known as the Tanzimat, which in Turkish means 'reorganisation'. For fifteen years the impetus for reform came from Mustafa Rashid Pasha (1800-1858) who had been the Ottoman ambassador to Paris and London in the 1830s. By the time of Mahmud II's death he was the empire's foreign minister. He would twice hold that position and would be Grand Vizier (*de facto* prime minister of the Ottoman Empire) six times. Rashid Pasha ensured the promotion of like-minded young men, who also wished to see the empire remodelled on a European basis. Two of these became very important in the reform movement, succeeding him as leader. Mehmed Emin Ali Pasha (1815-71), the son of a shopkeeper, was foreign minister under Rashid Pasha at the age of twenty-five. A year later he was appointed Ottoman ambassador to London and became Grand Vizier for the first of several times in 1852. He was assisted in his work for the last twenty years of the Tanzimat by Mehmed Fuad Pasha (1814-69) who served five terms as foreign minister. These three officials guided the empire through the Tanzimat years.

A few months after Mahmud II's death, Rashid Pasha issued a royal decree, the Hatt-i Sharif (Edict) of Gülhane, that launched the Tanzimat reform period. It promised certain administrative reforms – the ending of tax farming, the reform of the conscription system, the eradication of corruption and, somewhat remarkably, a guarantee of rights to every citizen of the Ottoman Empire no matter what his or her ethnic origins or religious persuasion were. The decree was intended to modernise the Ottoman Empire so that it would be able to compete with the major European powers. A second decree, the Hatt-i Humayun, was issued by Ali Pasha and Fuad Pasha in 1856, following the Crimean War. It re-emphasised these principles especially the one about the rights of all citizens. The aim of both decrees was to gain the loyalty of non-Muslim subjects in order to stave off growing nationalist sentiment in the provinces. They were unsuccessful even when followed in 1869 by a new Nationality Law that replaced religious affiliation with secular identity. Education also featured in the Tanzimat changes. New educational institutions were opened which provided an administrative elite that occupied senior positions in Turkey and in the Arab states well into the next century. In 1847, a Ministry of Education was established and a programme of secondary education – outside the control of the *ulama* – was proposed.

The justice system was completely revised during the Tanzimat, using the French civil code as the model. There were new penal and commercial codes and a new system of secular courts – *nizame* – was set up to deal with cases that involved Muslims and non-Muslims. The Mejelle civil code that was introduced, like so many of the reforms, combined both the traditional and the Western, although it was based on the *Shariah* and, therefore, unmistakeably Islamic.

During all this, Ottoman finances became a serious issue. The new programmes were expensive and state revenues were not increasing. The only way to pay for them, therefore, was to take out loans. In the twenty three years between 1854 and 1877, the Ottoman government borrowed more than 200 million Ottoman lire (around £180 million), forcing them to divert money from the empire's operating budget in order just to pay the interest on the loans. By 1874 around 60 per cent of the total expenditure of the Ottoman Empire went purely towards servicing the debt. Two years later, the government failed to make its payments, meaning, in effect, that the Ottoman Empire was bankrupt. European governments immediately took action to protect the creditors and the 1881 Decree of Muharram was negotiated whereby an Ottoman Public Debt Administration mechanism was created. It pledged to reserve certain state revenues to service the debt — effectively handing over Ottoman financial control to the Europeans. It would take until 1954 for the government of Turkey to finish repaying its debts.

The Crimean War

The Crimean War occurred partly as a result of Russian efforts to gain authority over the Greek Orthodox subjects of the empire who were treated as second-class citizens. For centuries, there had been issues over the rights of Christian minorities in the Holy Land, the French promoting the rights of Roman Catholics, and the Russians championing members of the Orthodox Church. In 1853, Russia demanded that the Ottoman government sign an accord guaranteeing the rights of its roughly 8 million Orthodox citizens. This would effectively have allowed the Russians to intervene in internal matters in the empire where Orthodox worshippers were involved. Understandably, the sultan rejected the demand. Russia responded by invading the Ottoman-controlled Danubian Principalities of Wallachia and Moldavia. Britain and France opposed and feared Russian expansion in the region. The British were particularly anxious that Russia might have ambitions to make advances towards India. Possible Russian expansion in the Baltic towards Scandinavia and other areas of Western Europe was also a concern.

The French and British intervention on the side of the Ottomans was symptomatic of efforts to maintain the balance of power in the east after the Treaty of Vienna of 1815. None of the powers was to be permitted to make territorial gains from the Ottoman Empire and the major European powers formed coalitions to maintain the status quo. The aim of such a policy was to prevent war over the Ottoman territories. In this case it failed and the Crimean War of 1853 to 1856 was fought between the Ottoman Empire, France and Great Britain in one corner and Russia in the other, and the theatre of war was the Russian territory of the Crimea. The war was won by the Ottoman, French and British coalition and ended with the 1856 Treaty of Paris by which the signatories agreed to respect the territorial integrity of the Ottoman Empire. The Black Sea was made neutral and warships were banned from its waters. The treaty represented a severe setback for Russian ambitions in the region but the war's legacy was one of nationalism, as many of the Balkan states began to agitate for autonomy.

Russia declared war on the Ottoman Empire again in 1877 during what became known as the Great Eastern Crisis. Anti-Ottoman rebellions erupted in Bosnia in 1875 and Bulgaria in 1876, although the Bulgarian revolt was suppressed swiftly and ruthlessly by the Ottomans. Russia, keen to support Balkan independence movements in order to secure influence in the region, responded with a declaration of war. The Ottomans were forced out of Bulgaria and, in 1878, the Russians captured Adrianople (modern day Edirne). Britain was preparing to go to war in order to protect its Middle Eastern ambitions when the German Chancellor Otto von Bismarck (1815-98) intervened, convening the Congress of Berlin to discuss the Ottoman Empire. In effect, the European powers used this conference to divide the empire up amongst themselves. The Ottomans lost Serbia, Montenegro, Romania and part of Bulgaria which all became independent. The eastern Anatolian regions of Kars and Batum were awarded to Russia while Austria was given Bosnia. Britain took Cyprus as a base to look after its interests in that part of the Mediterranean.

Ismail the Magnificent

The fifth governor of Egypt, Ismail (r. 1863-79), was the grandson of Muhammad Ali and a ruler on whom people are divided. However, his impact on Egypt both domestically and in its foreign relations endured well into the century after his death. 'My country,' he said, 'is no longer in Africa, it is now in Europe,' and he made great efforts to Europeanise Egypt. He encouraged Egyptians to be educated in Europe, and expanded education within the country, hugely increasing the budget devoted to it. Nonetheless, he remained an authoritarian ruler and, although he created a consultative chamber of delegates in 1866, he did not give it any real power. In relation to the Ottoman Empire, he used bribery and gifts to curry favour. It worked, as he was given the title *khedive* (viceroy) by Sultan Abdülaziz (r. 1861-76) who had been very well treated on a visit to Egypt.

Ismail introduced many other reforms. In 1876 he created the Mixed Courts to deal with disputes between Egyptians and foreigners living in the country. Under the Capitulations, such cases were heard by the consul of the foreigner and verdicts more often than not favoured him. Governed by the French civil code, these courts remained in existence until 1949. For deciding cases involving only Egyptians, the National Courts, drawing on the French civil code, were opened in 1884. *Shariah* courts continued but were now limited in their scope. Meanwhile, Egypt was becoming increasingly indebted, leading Ismail to try to increase revenue, introducing, for instance, the *muqabala* law that allowed landowners to pay six times their annual tax in return for being relieved of all future tax on their property. In 1875, he brought

£4 million into his coffers by selling Egypt's 44 per cent share in the Suez Canal to the British.

Ismail's reign ended after Egypt attempted to take a three-month debt holiday and he tried to sack two members of the Public Debt Commission that the European powers had imposed on the country. The Europeans petitioned the sultan to have him removed and he was replaced by his son Tewfik (r. 1879-92) in 1879.

The Urabi Revolt

Egypt now owed what was a staggering sum, for the time, of £98.4 million. The scale of Ismail's spending can be seen in the fact that when he assumed the throne the debt was a mere £3 million. But Tewfik regularised repayment, giving these repayments priority over all other expenditure and soon Egypt was on a more stable financial footing. Irritation with European interference in Egyptian affairs, however, soon erupted in open revolt led by a remarkable man, Ahmad Urabi (1841-1911). Born a peasant, Urabi attained the rank of colonel in the Egyptian army. He was not a 'French Knower' and was much liked by ordinary Egyptians. Soon he was at the head of a national movement, protesting against European influence over Egyptian affairs, which also wished to put restrictions on the khedive's powers. Urabi had the army on his side, as well as some 'notables' – prominent citizens – who wanted reform, and the peasants who saw him as the man who could ease their tax and debt burden. As Urabi became increasingly powerful, Tewfik increasingly relied on the European powers for support.

The British and French governments were fearful that the Urabists, if they came to power, would refuse to honour their financial obligations and that access to the Suez Canal would be restricted. When rioting broke out in Alexandria in June 1882, the commander of the British fleet anchored off the port was ordered to fire on the city. In August, a British expeditionary force landed on Egyptian soil and the following month scored a resounding victory over Urabi's army at the Battle of Tel el-Kebir. Fifty-seven British troops lost their lives but around 2,000 Egyptians died. Urabi was tried as a traitor and exiled. What had been viewed at the time by the British government as merely a brief action to support Tewfik turned into an occupation that was only ended by the Suez Crisis of 1956.

The Young Ottomans

There was a group of Turkish intellectuals who felt strongly that the Tanzimat reforms were not enough. Almost all of them had worked in the Ottoman Translation Bureau and were keenly aware of how European politics worked as well as the machinations of the Ottoman administration. They wanted to see change in the way that the empire interacted with the European powers but also in the style of government of the empire. At the same time, they wanted to retain the Islamic elements of their society. Their view of democracy was not the participatory style but, rather, consultation between an absolute ruler and the ministers he had appointed. They formed a secret society, Yeni Osmanlilar (Young Ottomans), but in 1867, after Namik Kemal (1840-88) and others published an open letter from Egyptian Prince Mustafa Fazil Pasha (1830-75) to Sultan Abdülaziz, advocating a constitutional and parliamentary style of government, they were forced to flee into exile in Paris. They advertised their dissent in a number of widely circulated publications, one of the most important of which was *Hürriyet* (Liberty).

THE OTTOMAN EMPIRE AFTER 1800

The new Sultan Abdul Hamid II (r. 1876-1909) promulgated a new constitution for the empire which made provisions for a parliament but he went on to dismiss this parliament after about five months. It would be thirty years before it would convene again.

However, constitutionalism in the region was on the rise as was demonstrated in Iran in 1906 when the shah was forced to call a national assembly and accept a liberal constitution. In 1908, a group of Ottoman army officers — known to history as the Young Turks — forced the reluctant sultan to reintroduce the constitution of 1876 and the Ottoman Empire once again began to savour constitutional and parliamentary government.

A New Middle East

Lord Cromer and the British Occupation of Egypt (1882-1914)

By the late nineteenth century, the major European nations were all-powerful, securing their possessions with agreements amongst themselves and dividing the world up between them as they pleased. Britain was particularly busy, establishing treaties with Arab sheiks in the Persian Gulf and annexing Aden in order to keep the route to India safe. Bahrain signed an exclusive agreement with Britain in 1880, Muscat in 1891 and Kuwait in 1899. In 1881, France occupied Tunisia, adding it to its French North African Empire. Morocco would follow in 1912. Italy, desperate for its own place in the sun, invaded the Ottoman province of Tripoli in 1911. The rivalry between the superpowers had a great impact on the nations of the Middle East, especially Egypt, Iran and Sudan.

Egypt remained an enigma in the British Empire. It had not been declared a colony or a protectorate and was, of course, still an autonomous province of the Ottoman Empire. The man who ran it for the next quarter of a century was a colonial administrator who had already served in India. Evelyn Baring, later Lord Cromer (1841–1917), was appointed Consul-General of Egypt in 1883, charged with the introduction of minor reforms and the withdrawal of British troops. He had to make Egypt's debt repayments a priority and ensure the position of the khedive. Cromer was a typical British colonial administrator, convinced of the superiority of the West and the inability of nations of the Middle East and the East to develop without the help of countries like his. To his mind, it would be a long time before Egypt could be allowed to be self-determining. He was determined to prevent the country from developing any industry that might prove a threat to British industry and therefore concentrated on improving agriculture, creating better irrigation and approving significant projects such as the construction of the Aswan Dam which was completed in 1902. There was also considerable investment in Egypt's already large railway network. His work only helped to increase Egyptian dependence on the export of cotton.

By the mid-1880s, there were signs of success. Egypt showed a healthy surplus and debts were being repaid. There was a cost, however, and many of Ismail's educational institutions closed. Cromer also introduced tuition fees that severely restricted access to education to those who could afford it. He was opposed to the education of ordinary people, considering it inevitable that, once educated, they would become frustrated with their place in the scheme of things, thus creating nationalist feeling and unrest.

The issue of Sudan encouraged the British to keep a presence in Egypt. Sudan had been finally conquered by Ismail but a remarkable man, Muhammad Ahmad (1844-85) – popularly known as the Mahdi – emerged. The Mahdi was the term for a much-prophesied, messianic leader of the Islamic faith and this man proclaimed himself to be that person. In 1881, he led a rebellion in Sudan against Egyptian occupation, defeating both an Egyptian force and General Gordon (1833-85) at Khartoum in 1885. The Mahdi died later that year, but, mainly because of the cost of intervention, the British and Egyptians left Sudan to his supporters for the next ten years. By the 1890s, however, the 'scramble for Africa' was well and truly under way with the European powers grabbing every piece of the continent they could. Suspicious that the French might be about to seize Sudan, the British government dispatched an Anglo-Egyptian expeditionary force under General Herbert Kitchener (1850-1916). Sudan was conquered by 1898 but, instead of being returned to Egyptian control, was taken over by Britain with a British Governor-General installed to run it. The Egyptians were, naturally, outraged and would remain so for decades. Their ire only ended in 1955 when the Sudanese voted for independence rather than amalgamation with Egypt.

Opposition to the British increased after Cromer resigned in 1907. He was succeeded as Consul-General by Sir Eldon Gorst (1861-1911) and General Kitchener who governed from Gorst's death in 1911 to the outbreak of the First World War in 1914. Each made efforts to placate the Egyptians but anti-British sentiment continued. Finally, the last khedive, Abbas II (r. 1892-1914), who had secretly been supporting the Egyptian nationalist movement led by lawyer and journalist Mustafa Kamil (1874-1908), was deposed in 1914. Ismail the Magnificent's son, Hussein Kamel (r. 1914-17), was declared Sultan of Egypt and Egypt became a British Protectorate, bringing to an end Ottoman sovereignty which had been in place since 1517.

Iran in the Second Half of the Nineteenth Century

Between the end of the Safavid dynasty in 1722 and the arrival of the Qajar dynasty 74 years later, Iran (historically referred to as Persia by westerners) was in turmoil, lacking any central government. This, at least, kept the Europeans at bay slightly longer than in Egypt. Initially, the Qajars succeeded in driving the Russians out of the entire Caucasus but two wars against them, from 1804 to 1813 and from 1826 to 1828, brought large territorial losses to Iran including Transcaucasia and Dagestan which had been under Iranian control for three centuries.

The Qajars were seen by the Shiite religious elite as merely temporal rulers, without the religious authority of the Safavid shahs who were seen as divinely inspired. The *ulama*, therefore, claimed the right to adjudicate on legal and religious matters. The previously close relationship between Shia Islam and the state ended, and the religious establishment gained new independence and power in Iran, often opposing the decisions of the shah.

Establishing their capital at Teheran, the Qajar shahs lived in extravagant luxury and gave the appearance of possessing great authority, but sometimes their rule extended little further than the gates of their capital. Most of the plum jobs went to family members and semi-autonomous local chieftains. There was little chance, therefore, of an efficient, professional bureaucracy emerging. Bribery and corruption became the norm and unregulated landlords exploited the peasantry. Meanwhile, the religious establishment maintained its independence from the government, benefitting from donations while the shah struggled for revenue. The money went into establishing *madrasas* (religious schools) and helping the poor. The clerics' influence over the population grew as a result and they appeared to be providing greater protection to the Persian people than the government.

Russia and Britain soon began to exert influence over Iran. The Russians defeated the shah's forces in 1828 and imposed the Treaty of Turkmenchay that gave their merchants similarly beneficial rights to those enjoyed by Western European powers in the Ottoman Empire's Capitulations. Britain became concerned that the Russians were beginning to pose a threat to their interests in India and Russian industry would, of course, be a threat to British commercial ambitions. Therefore, they sought and obtained rights equivalent to those of the Russians. So, in the face of competition from cheap foreign imports, the Iranian textile industry declined. Shah Nasir al-Din (r. 1848-96) played the two powers off against one another in order to acquire much needed revenue and before long his court was swamped with Europeans seeking concessions. The exploitation of the two powers, however, created problems and sometimes nothing was achieved. By 1900, for instance, Iran had only twenty miles of railway.

The corruption and inefficiency of the Iranian government inevitably led to trouble. In 1900, the granting to a British company of the rights to produce, sell and export the Iranian tobacco crop brought mass protests, led by the *ulama*. A boycott of tobacco was ordered by the religious leaders and eventually, in the face of more protests, the shah was forced to cancel the concession. Borrowing from Russia to remain solvent, Iran slipped into debt, like the Ottoman Empire and Egypt, and became increasingly isolated. Shah Nasir al-Din forbade the construction of new schools and prohibited his subjects from travelling to Europe. When he was assassinated in 1896, he was not widely mourned by his people.

Thus, by the end of the century, the Europeans exerted control over almost the entire Middle East. If countries were not occupied their sovereignties and economies were controlled and limited from outside their borders. This, of course, presented a religious dilemma for Muslims who concluded that it was not Islam that was at fault, but Muslims themselves. Thinkers and political activists argued that the 'French knowers' – those educated in the West – were responsible for the failure to observe Islamic practices, having abandoned the *Shariah* for laws made by man and not by God.

There was a growing resentment and rejection of European institutions and practices and an increased desire for a return to Islamic values.

Sultan Abdul Hamid II (r. 1876-1909)

When Abdul Hamid II arrived on the Ottoman throne in 1876, he quickly seized control of the government machinery from the bureaucrats, restoring autocratic rule. By the end of his reign, he was oppressively acting against European institutions and interests as well as against his own subjects, restricting their intellectual and political activity. The press was censored and political discussion in public was banned. The regime's spies and informers penetrated every level of society and the government, and intellectuals and officials were exiled or imprisoned, often on the flimsiest of evidence. Universities and colleges became hotbeds of discontent and those exiled denounced the sultan and his regime from afar in materials smuggled into the empire. Separatist movements were ruthlessly suppressed, especially the Armenians who were agitating for the creation of an independent Armenian Christian state in Anatolia. In 1909, in an act of genocide, Abdul Hamid sent Kurdish irregulars into Armenian villages where countless innocent people were massacred. When he used the same tactics to suppress an uprising in Crete a horrified Greek government declared war on the Ottoman Empire. The empire won easily but the European powers forced a reluctant sultan to accept Crete's autonomy.

Abdul Hamid returned to the trappings of the pre-Tanzimat empire and befriended the religious elite. The notion of religious equality across the empire was consigned to history and, instead, he introduced the doctrine of Pan-Islamism. He was unlikely to be able to convert all his subjects to Islam but it was good for his image and helped him in his quest to throw off European domination. It was also of benefit in his dealings with the Europeans, allowing him to persuade them that he exerted control over the millions of Muslims in the Ottoman Empire. His concept of Pan-Islamism was manifested most clearly in the construction of the Hijaz railway that ran from Damascus to Medina. Opened in 1908, it was paid for by Muslims around the world, not a penny of European money going towards it. As well as facilitating the pilgrimage of Muslims to the holy shrine, the railway also provided the empire with a swift method of transporting troops to Western Arabia, bypassing the Suez Canal. He supervised a rapid expansion of the empire's road and rail network. In 1883, a railway link was opened between Istanbul and Vienna and the famous Orient Express soon began plying the route between the Ottoman capital and Paris. An extensive telegraph network connected the most distant parts of the empire, helping the government to exercise control over its outlying provinces.

The transport connection with Europe fostered a relationship with Germany and a German general, Colmar von der Goltz (1843-1916), was appointed to reorganise the Ottoman army. Kaiser Wilhelm II (r. 1888-1918) visited the empire twice, in 1889 and 1898, declaring Germany to be a friend to the world's 300 million Muslims. In 1910, after a request for a loan from both Britain and France had been unsuccessful, the Ottomans secured it from Germany and the sultan declared it to be 'consistent with the dignity of Turkey', unlike the conditions the other two European nations had wanted to impose. The Berlin to Baghdad railway line, built with German money, was of concern to the British but a compromise was reached that made the railway line acceptable. However, it was a victory for German imperialists who had championed the notion of the 'Drang nach Osten' (push to the east).

In Europe, the naval and military arms race was underway and Turkey increasingly gravitated towards Berlin. It has to be remembered that the British in Lower Iraq and the French in Syria were encroaching on the empire's territory. Meanwhile, the Russians were encouraging Balkan, Kurdish and Armenian nationalist movements. In 1913, General Liman von Sanders (1855-1929) was sent to Istanbul to reorganise the Turkish armed forces, partly in response to the French military mission to Russia in the same year which was led by General Joseph Joffre (1852-1931). German military staff were brought in amid a torrent of protest from the powers of the Triple Entente – Great Britain, France and Russia. The Turks reminded them, however, that the Turkish police were trained by the French, the navy had been trained by the British and that there had been a decades-long military connection with Germany. After the Austro-Hungarian Archduke Franz Ferdinand (1863-1914) was assassinated, precipitating the rush towards the First World War, Turkey was admitted into the Triple Alliance alongside Germany, Austria-Hungary and Italy.

The Young Turks

As we have seen, there was an active dissident community in exile, operating in Paris and Geneva. From afar they condemned Abdul Hamid II's autocratic regime and demanded the restoration of the 1876 constitution but they had little chance of achieving their aims and often argued amongst themselves. There was also growing opposition to Abdul Hamid within the Ottoman Empire. A secret society known as the Committee of Union and Protest (CUP) was founded by students of the military-medical academy in 1889. In common with the foreign-based dissidents, they were products of the European-style educational institutions and believed the empire could be preserved only with the end of Abdul Hamid's reign and reforms. In the mid-1890s, however, the CUP fell victim to the sultan's intricate spy network, and many of its members were arrested and exiled. Further repressive measures limited the scope of the opposition.

As Abdul Hamid's reign drew to a close, the army was suffering from poor equipment and unpaid salaries. Officers formed opposition groups that aligned with the CUP. In the summer of 1908, a group of officers of the Third Army based in Salonika revolted, demanding the reintroduction of the 1876 constitution and threatening to march on Istanbul if the sultan did not acquiesce to their demands. Abdul Hamid hastily restored the constitution. For a time everyone rallied behind this and, by the end of the year, the sultan had reconvened the Chamber of Deputies he had abolished thirty years previously. But the new government was too European for some and there was an uprising the following spring by soldiers and theological students who called for the reinstatement of the *Shariah*. The Third Army responded by marching on Istanbul to put down the rebellion. As it was believed Abdul Hamid had encouraged the rebellion, the Chamber of Deputies decided to depose him. He was exiled to Salonika and his younger brother Mehmet V (r. 1909-18) replaced him, although he enjoyed little power.

For the next four years there was a battle for power between the CUP, consisting of junior army officers and civil servants on one side, and groups made up of liberals and conservatives who opposed them. By 1913, the CUP were in control of the government, ruling in what was, in effect, a military dictatorship headed by Ismail Enver (1881-1922), Mehmed Talaat (1874-1921) and Ahmed Djemal (Jamal) (1872-1922). Enver and Jamal were alumni of the war college in Istanbul who had been staff officers of the Third Army in Salonika, and Talaat had risen from humble origins to become the empire's grand vizier. In the beginning it was an exhilarating time. The restrictions on the press were lifted, educational provision was improved and the neglected armed forces were updated. Corrupt officials were pensioned off and there were cutbacks in the civil service. But this antagonised those employed by the state as well as many important Arab families whose posts in the provincial administration had been almost a matter of birthright.

The new government had to maintain the Islamic legitimacy of the empire and therefore reinstated the sultan's role as the caliph. It was a difficult balancing act, doing away with the religious differences between Muslim rulers and their non-Muslim subjects and discouraging nationalist movements within the empire. And ultimately it proved impossible. In 1908, Bulgaria declared itself independent, Austria annexed Bosnia, and Crete became part of Greece. In 1911, Italy invaded Tripoli, flouting Ottoman sovereignty over the region and, the following year, the empire had to sign a treaty that ceded Tripoli and several of the Dodecanese islands to the Italians. That same year, Albania declared independence and the First Balkan War broke out. An alliance of Bulgaria, Serbia, Greece and Montenegro drove the Ottomans out of much of Europe. They regained Thrace afterwards but their territory in Europe shrank from 65,350 square miles and 6.1 million people in 1912 to 10,882 square miles and 1.9 million people by September 1913.

The heart of the empire – Anatolian Turkey – now became key and, indeed, a specifically Turkish cultural movement began to emerge. It had two elements. Pan-Turkism emphasised the links between all speakers of Turkish. This took in people who lived in various places between Anatolia and China – Turkish-speakers in Russia, Afghanistan, Iran and China. The second element, Turkism, was, however, much more topical. It stressed the Turkish core of the Ottoman Empire, going back to the pre-Ottoman and pre-Islamic heritage of the empire. It was the beginning of the separation of Turkey from Ottomanism and laid the foundations for the Turkish nationalist movement that would erupt after the First World War.

Iran's Constitutional Revolution

It was also a time of change in Iran. The period between 1905 and 1911 in Iran is remembered as the period of constitutional revolution, undertaken by an unwieldy coalition of merchants, the religious elite and a group of reformist radicals. Each of these was convinced that with constitutional government and restrictions on the shah's powers, it could govern the country correctly.

Once again a shah – Mozaffar ad-Din (r. 1896-1907) – was in need of funds and, as well as borrowing heavily from European banks, he gave oil rights in all but five provinces to the British businessman William D'Arcy (1849-1917) in exchange for 16 per cent of the annual profits. In 1908, substantial quantities of oil were discovered and six years later the British government became the major shareholder in the company to which the concession had been granted. The preservation of its Iranian oil interests became central to British Middle East policy.

The protest movement began in December 1905 and, by October 1906, the shah was forced to sign a decree convening a constituent assembly. When it met it totally restructured politics in Iran. The shah's powers were limited and final authority over all economic matters was allocated to the elected legislature. The rights of Iranian citizens were defined and the legislature was given the right to appoint and dismiss ministers. 'Twelver'

Shi'ism was declared the official religion of the state and new legislation was to be reviewed by a committee of scholars to ensure that it conformed to the strictures of the *Shariah*. The new shah, Muhammad Ali Shah (1907-09), reluctantly signed the decree.

At this moment, Britain and Russia signed an agreement that divided Iran between them as spheres of influence. Britain would control the southeast of the country and Russia would have the north while the central area would remain neutral. The Iranian people were horrified by their loss of sovereignty, the shah seizing the opportunity to re-establish royal authority in the capital. Civil war and economic chaos broke out, lasting almost a year, the shah holding on to the capital, but failing to reassert his authority over the rest of the country. In summer 1909, an armed force of rebels marched on Teheran and restored the constitution, deposing the shah and replacing him with his young son who took the throne under a regent. Still there was no peace, however, and there were armed clashes between supporters of the various political groupings in the Majlis (parliament). Once again, in the provinces the tribal confederations reasserted their independence, and law and order broke down. In October 1911, increasingly concerned at the deteriorating situation in its sphere of influence and worried about its oil interests, Britain landed troops at Bushehr and occupied their section of Iran. The Russians did likewise in the north, threatening to invade Teheran if a newly appointed American financial adviser was not removed from office. When the Majlis refused, it was immediately dissolved by the prime minister and his cabinet. He and a group of conservative ministers now governed Iran, supervised closely by Britain and Russia. The activities of the two occupying powers in their territories were carried out independently of Teheran. Thus, the efforts of the coalition of merchants, religious leaders and reformers to remove foreign influence from their country had only resulted in an even more divided Iran and one even more in thrall to foreigners.

The First World War and the Fall of the Ottoman Empire

The First World War in the Middle East

As Europe drifted inexorably towards war, the Ottoman Empire remained neutral. Arab nationalists – the secret societies al-Ahd and al-Fatat – remained cautious, exhorting people to support Turkey against foreign penetration. Britain, through Kitchener and his Oriental Secretary Ronald Storrs (1881-1955), had been communicating with the Sharif Hussein bin Ali of Mecca (1879-1935) who ruled the Holy Cities and resented the centralising efforts of the sultan that would have him reporting to a Turkish official responsible to Istanbul. He had solicited the help of the British who, in October 1914, made a commitment in principle to the 'emancipation of the Arabs' and the creation of an 'Arab nation' if the Arabs would commit themselves to the Allied cause in the forthcoming conflict. There was even encouragement to stage an Arab revolt against the Ottoman Empire. Eventually, the Arabs agreed to stage a revolt after the British government announced that it would recognise an independent Arab kingdom that was made up of Arabia (excluding Aden), Palestine, Syria and Iraq. The British were unaware of the existence of the secret societies and believed, rather, that the notion of a Greater Arab nation belonged principally to the Sharif and was a manifestation of his own personal ambition. A famous correspondence on the subject began – the Hussein-McMahon correspondence – between the Sharif and Sir Henry McMahon (1862-1949), British High Commissioner in Egypt.

In spring 1916, a Turkish force with German officers was sent as reinforcements to Turkish troops in Yemen who had succeeded in forcing the small British garrison guarding the Aden Protectorate to pull back to the Aden Colony. Using the Hijaz railway, the Turks arrived in Medina in May, alarming the Sharif who feared that they had discovered his correspondence with the British. He was out of favour with the Ottomans and was aware that he would be deposed at the conclusion of the war. His son, Faisal (r. Syria 1920; Iraq 1921-33), learning of executions of Arab nationalists by the Ottoman governor in Syria, decided that there was no point in delaying the revolt. It was launched on 5 June 1916, the Sharif accusing the Young Turks of violating Islam. It would prove invaluable to British forces in the Middle East theatre, preventing a Turkish-German attack on the Suez Canal. Its importance was described after the war by Lord Wavell (1883-1950):

'Its value to the British commander was great, since it diverted considerable Turkish reinforcements and supplies to the Hijaz, and protected the right flank of the British armies in their advance through Palestine. Further, it put an end to German propaganda in southwestern Arabia and removed any danger of the establishment of a German submarine base on the Red Sea. These were important services, and worth the subsidies in gold and munitions expended on the Arab forces.'

Don Peretz, *The Middle East Today*,
Praeger, Santa Barbara, 1994

Arab forces numbered around 5,000 but there were also irregular forces fighting under the command of the British army officer, archaeologist and diplomat T.E. Lawrence (1888-1935) – 'Lawrence of Arabia' – and Faisal. Arabs would also join the campaign sporadically when it impinged upon their own home region. By 1918 it is estimated that Faisal's forces may have amounted to around 30,000 men and the British were spending around £220,000 a month to subsidise the revolt. Ottoman troops numbered around 20,000 by 1917 and there was also support from the Ottoman air force as well as planes and pilots from Germany. But the revolt failed to raise the civilian populations of the empire's Arab provinces in revolt partly because of the success of the repressive measures in Syria.

Meanwhile, in Iraq, the Indian Army authorities, who were in control, made sure that local Arabs knew nothing of the uprising because they did not want to encourage ideas of independence. They also feared that the revolt might cause unrest amongst India's ninety million Muslims. Nonetheless, the Arab Revolt, continuing throughout the war, stirred in the minds of Arabs aspirations that would be addressed immediately after the conflict.

The Ottomans joined the Central powers through the secret Ottoman-German Alliance, signed on 2 August 1914. They were focused on regaining the territories they had lost in the war with Russia of 1877-78 while the Germans wanted to cut off Russian and British access to the oil resources around the Caspian Sea. The possibility of the Germans capturing oilfields in the Middle East represented a great threat to the British as the Royal Navy depended upon oil from southern Iran. The Russians, meanwhile, were seeking a postwar settlement that gave them the Ottoman capital, the Bosphorus, the Dardanelles, the Sea of Marmara, southern Thrace and sectors of the Black Sea coast of Anatolia. The Armenians joined on the Allied side with a view to establishing an Armenian state. This was achieved in May 1918 with the First Republic of Armenia, although it did not last long.

In the Caucasus, the Ottomans faced Allied forces plus troops from Azerbaijan, Armenia and the Central Caspian Dictatorship – a short-lived anti-Soviet entity in the city of Baku. The campaign stretched from the Caucasus to eastern Asia Minor and there was also action by the Russian Navy in the Black Sea. It ended with the Treaty of Brest-Litovsk, signed with Russia and the Treaty of Batum signed with Armenia. In the first of these treaties, signed on 3 March 1918, Russia's new Bolshevik government withdrew from the war, reneging on all its commitments to the Triple Entente alliance. The Baltic States were ceded to Germany and the Ottoman Empire gained the province of Kars Oblast in the southern Caucasus. Russia was also forced to pay huge reparations.

In the Sinai and Palestine campaign the British faced the Ottomans and the Germans. The Ottomans, led by German commanders, tried to capture the Suez Canal in 1915 but were forced to retreat. The British Desert Column recaptured the Sinai in January 1917 and won the First and Second Battles of Gaza in southern Palestine. In October 1917, General Edmund Allenby (1861-1936) won a number of victories, gaining territory but in 1918 when a number of his troops were sent to the Western Front after the successful German Spring Offensive, he failed to capture Amman and halted his advance. New troops from Australia, New Zealand, India and South Africa led to the resumption of operations and his force succeeded in breaching the Ottoman lines and capturing more territory, prisoners and equipment. Following the capture of Damascus and Aleppo, the Armistice of Mudros, signed on 30 October 1918, ended the Sinai and Palestine Campaign. It was a campaign little trumpeted around the world but it would have long-lasting implications for the Middle East as the British Mandate of Palestine and the French Mandate for Syria and Lebanon were created as a result of it.

The brutal Gallipoli Campaign was fought in the Gallipoli peninsula between 25 April 1915 and 9 January 1916. The Dardanelles Strait provided a sea route to the Russian Empire and to secure it the Allies launched a naval attack and an amphibious troop landing. The objective was the capture of the Ottoman capital Constantinople but the naval attack failed and, after eight months of vicious fighting, famously involving the ANZAC forces of Australia and New Zealand, with more than half a million casualties, the Ottoman forces recorded one of the war's greatest victories. It represented a defining moment in Turkish history, the last gasp battle for the survival of the empire. It set off the catalogue of events that resulted in the declaration of the Republic of Turkey eight years later, headed by Mustafa Kemal (1881-1938) who had been an officer of the Turkish army at Gallipoli.

In Mesopotamia, British, Indian and Australian troops faced mostly Ottoman troops. The British sought to protect their oil interests while also defending the approaches to India. The Germans and the Ottomans wanted to liberate Persia from foreign control and create a wedge between the Russians and the British that would open the way to British India, Azerbaijan and Central Asia. Late in 1914, Major General Sir Charles Townshend (1861-1924) led a force of 25,000 British and Indian troops to protect the oil installations at Abadan at the mouth of the Shatt-al-Arab strait and to prevent the Turks from advancing towards the Suez Canal. All went well initially, and the town of Kut-al-Amara was taken on 26 September 1915 before an advance on Baghdad began. After a year of setbacks, however, the Turks had strengthened their forces and their resolve. Two days of hard fighting in the Battle of Ctesiphon halted the Allied advance. Townshend hastily led his force back to Kut where they were besieged for five awful months by an Ottoman force led by the German Field Marshal Baron von der Goltz. Townshend surrendered on 29 April 1916 and 5,000 of the 13,000 survivors of the siege later died of disease or were killed by their Ottoman guards while they were captives. It was a humiliating episode for the British and provided a huge morale boost for the Turkish army.

Major General Stanley Maude (1864-1917) took command of the British army in Mesopotamia, leading the capture of Baghdad in March 1917, at the same time seizing the Berlin-Baghdad railway. British forces, as well as the Russians who were closing in from the north and east, made great advances against the Turks. The British defeated them in Palestine, but the conflict continued into the following year until the signing of the Armistice of Mudros.

The armistice agreement forced the Ottomans to surrender their remaining garrisons outside Anatolia and the Allies were given the right to occupy the forts that controlled the Dardanelles and the Bosphorus, as well as to occupy any Ottoman territory 'in case of disorder' or where there was a perceived threat to security. The Ottoman armed forces were demobilised and the Allies given full use of all ports, railways and other important facilities. British, French and Italian forces occupied Constantinople and remained there until 23 September 1923. It was the first time that Constantinople had fallen into foreign hands since its capture by the Turks in 1453.

The Partitioning of the Ottoman Empire

France and Britain now sought the dismemberment of the Ottoman territories, partitioning it into small political entities. The partitioning was planned throughout the First World War in a series of agreements, most significantly the Sykes-Picot Agreement. This secret agreement between the governments of Britain and France had the assent of Russia and defined the major powers' proposed spheres of influence after a successful conclusion to the war. Concluded on 16 May 1916, it was the work of Sir Mark Sykes (1879-1919) and François Georges-Picot (1870-1951) who divided the Ottoman Empire's Arab provinces into areas of British or French control.

In January 1919, twenty-seven nations convened in Paris to devise a peace settlement that would guarantee no future wars. The Middle East proved difficult and it would not be until the settlement agreed at the San Remo Conference of April 1920 – reluctantly signed by the government of the Ottoman Empire in August of that year – that issues would finally be settled. Ottoman sovereignty was seriously restricted. The straits between the Black Sea and the Mediterranean were to be governed by an international commission; France, Italy and Greece were awarded spheres of influence in southern Anatolia; and Greece took over Thrace, the last Ottoman province in Europe. At the time, national self-determination was the buzzword but the victorious nations only applied it when it suited them.

At San Remo, the Ottoman's Arab provinces were detached from the former empire, allocated to either Britain or France and called Mandates. Effectively, this was just a way of dressing up old-fashioned imperialism. Britain was given the Mandates for Iraq and Palestine and France was given the Mandate for Syria. The brand new state of Iraq was formed from three former Ottoman provinces – Basra, Baghdad and Mosul. These three were thrown together, although they had little to unify them. It was important to Britain, however, in that it gave her control of the approaches to British India and access to all-important oil reserves in the region.

Meanwhile, matters were complicated further by the British Foreign Secretary, Arthur James Balfour (1848-1930). In a letter of 2 November 1917 to Walter Rothschild, 2nd Baron Rothschild, a prominent British Zionist, he had made a case for a Jewish state in Palestine. It would become known as the Balfour Declaration and would be incorporated into the 1920 Treaty of Sèvres. He wrote:

> 'His Majesty's government view with favour the establishment in Palestine of a national home for the Jewish people, and will use their best endeavours to facilitate the achievement of this object, it being clearly understood that nothing shall be done which may prejudice the civil and religious rights of existing non-Jewish communities in Palestine, or the rights and political status enjoyed by Jews in any other country.'
>
> Yapp, ME, *The Making of the Modern Middle East 1792-1923*,
> Longman, Harlow, 1988

Faisal's Short-Lived Syrian Kingdom

While the Allies were dividing up the world in Paris, Amir Faisal was establishing an Arab government in Damascus. The young activists, former Ottoman officials and army officers who were involved in this venture dreamt of a united Syria and Palestine and prominent Syrians and leaders of the Arab Revolt, who felt they deserved some political reward for their efforts, also entered the mix of factions jostling for power. In March 1920, Syria was proclaimed an independent state with Faisal as its king. Of course, this went against French claims on Syria guaranteed by their clandestine wartime agreement with Britain. To hold the various agreements together, Britain had to agree at San Remo to assign the Mandate over Syria to France. Naturally, Arab nationalists were horrified and many urged Faisal to defy the Allies. Others counselled caution, hoping to be able to satisfy French demands but arrive at a compromise that would maintain the new Syrian kingdom. Even though Faisal offered to negotiate, French troops marched on Syria and, on 24 July 1920, easily defeated his army and occupied Damascus. Faisal had no option but to flee into exile in Europe. The Syrian state – the independent Arab state discussed during the war – had lasted a mere five months.

In one last desperate throw of the dice, Faisal's brother, Abdullah (1882-1951), led a force from Mecca to the desert town of Ma'an, east of the Jordan River. The British were under no particular threat from this action but were aware of Abdullah's power to unify the region's dissident tribes. It was decided, therefore, to bring him into the imperial fold. He was offered the chance to establish an administration, guided by Britain, in Amman. It would be added to the British Mandate over Palestine but would not be subject to the terms of the Balfour Declaration. He accepted and in 1921, Transjordan was created.

Meanwhile, the Arabs were undoubtedly bitter towards the Allies, harbouring a sense of understandable betrayal. It led to years of suspicion and a sense of what-might-have-been regarding the Arab state.

For four hundred years the lives of millions of people in the Middle East had been defined by the Ottoman Empire. It had been a remarkable regime that had adapted as necessary, governing directly where necessary but also allowing a degree of autonomy to local chieftains where it was suitable. Cooperation was the name of the game, religious and cultural toleration were often exercised and it maintained the *status quo* admirably for centuries. The Ottoman state provided security and stable government and it also provided a social order founded on the notions of *Shariah* justice, a respect for the *ulama* and the protection of the holy shrines of Islam. It provided hope that an Islamic state could persevere in a world where the major European powers called the shots. By 1920, it had all been washed away.

The new order of the postwar successor states would be less tolerant and less accommodating. Strict central control would be imposed on remote tribes and cultures and peoples.

Between the Wars

New States

It had all been so simple before the outbreak of the First World War. During the nineteenth and early twentieth centuries, the Middle East was controlled by three entities – Egypt, the Ottoman Empire and Iran. Gradually, of course, the rapacious European powers had begun to make inroads but power remained in the hands of those governing from Cairo, Istanbul and Teheran. Following the war, the Ottoman Empire was broken up into six states – Turkey and the five new Middle Eastern Arab states of Syria, Lebanon, Palestine, Iraq and late arrival Transjordan. Saudi Arabia and Yemen were now also seen as distinct political entities. But European influence remained all-powerful. Indeed, it could be said that of the ten most important Middle Eastern states, only four – Turkey, Iran, Yemen and Saudi Arabia – operated as fully sovereign states between the wars. And, in fact, Yemen and Saudi Arabia were allowed to function as sovereign states largely because Britain and France regarded them as remote and unimportant. Turkey would be the only new state that managed to steer its own path in foreign and domestic matters during this time.

The newly created League of Nations gave its blessing to the new states and France and Britain's administration of them as

Mandates. The rather patronising reason given by the League was that the Mandates 'were inhabited by peoples not yet able to stand by themselves under the strenuous conditions of the modern world'. They were to be assisted by what the League described as 'advanced nations' until such time as they were 'able to stand alone'. Of course, this implied that Britain and France were going to be readying these countries to govern themselves independently of outside forces. This was, of course, far from the reality and they were merely being allowed to pursue their own imperial interests. Still, there was at least an expectation that the Mandates would end at some point.

The Arabs in these fledgling states spent the inter-war years focused not on land reform, social welfare legislation or other socially beneficial programmes. Rather, they concentrated their energies on eliminating foreign control and achieving independence. Unfortunately, the same elite that had been in place in Egypt, Palestine, Syria and Lebanon was still there after the war and they continued to benefit from their positions throughout the inter-war years. In Iraq, it was former Ottoman officers who became the ruling class and they behaved no differently to the Ottoman ruling elite prior to 1914. It was a situation of compromise, however, because as they worked against Britain or France, they also depended on those two powers for their positions. They made strenuous efforts, therefore, not to upset them.

Economically, of course, the situation became very complex. In the place of one state with an economy run from Constantinople by the imperial authority, there were now a number of states with their own economic interests, customs tariffs and regulations. And each, of course, enjoyed a different economic relationship with the European power that supervised its actions. There were those who argued that each state should be able to carve out its own personal cultural and national identity while others still espoused the notion of pan-Arab unity and entreated the rulers of the individual nations to sacrifice their local power to the idea of Islamic solidarity and an Arab confederation.

Post-War Turkey and the Atatürk Era

In Istanbul after the war, with the CUP leadership having fled and the Allies in control, the only authority left was Sultan Mehmed VI (r. 1918-22) who had dissolved the Ottoman parliament and chosen to rule by decree. He had also chosen to cooperate with the occupiers of his land, opening himself to charges of collaboration. But the Treaty of Sèvres had severely punished the Ottomans and even in territory that was unoccupied or not under Allied control, the Sultan's powers were limited. Soon, however, the treaty would be rendered redundant by events.

Naturally, local resistance groups formed against the occupiers – societies for the defence of rights, as they described themselves – and these were soon operating as guerrilla bands under the leadership of experienced former Ottoman soldiers. One of these was Mustafa Kemal, born in Salonika into a Muslim, Turkish-speaking, middle-class family. Kemal joined the army and fought in the Italo-Turkish War of 1911-1912, the Balkan Wars of 1912-1913 and the First World War, serving with great distinction as a front-line commander at Gallipoli as well as on the eastern and Syrian fronts. He had become involved with the CUP, opposing Sultan Abdul Hamid, but had dissociated himself from the regressive policies of the Young Turk regime. Soon known as a nationalist leader, he was dismissed from the army but other officers began to join his cause. Determined to replace the government in Istanbul, Kemal convened a meeting of nationalists from Anatolia and Thrace in Ankara in spring of 1920 and, on 23

April, they decided to form a government with Mustafa Kemal at its head. In January of the following year, a constitution was proclaimed that contained the National Pact, renouncing claims on any of the territories of its former empire and affirming full Turkish sovereignty over areas of the former empire that were occupied by a Turkish majority. This included the Anatolian territory that had been granted to the new Armenian state. Thus, in autumn 1920, Turkey and the Soviet Union invaded Armenia and divided the territory between them. This action helped to cement the good relations between Turkey and the Soviet Union which meant that the Turks no longer needed to feel threatened by their giant eastern neighbour and could concentrate, instead, on the threat posed by Greece to the west.

In 1921, both the USSR and France recognised Kemal's Ankara government and the Italians, who had been occupying southern Anatolia since the end of the war, withdrew their troops. Turkey forced the Greeks into retreat in the Battle of Sakarya and Kemal took Izmir the following year before turning his attention to occupied Istanbul, determined to enforce the conditions of the National Pact. Before the situation deteriorated into conflict, both sides agreed to negotiate. The Armistice of Mudanya was signed on 11 October 1922 by Turkey, Greece and Great Britain. By this agreement, Greece was to withdraw from Turkish territory it had captured and the now defunct Treaty of Sèvres would be renegotiated at a conference.

Although Britain invited both the Ankara and Istanbul governments to the conference, Kemal wrong-footed them in November 1922 by introducing legislation in his parliament to abolish the sultanate. Instead, the caliphate would become a purely religious office. Mehmed VI, the last of six centuries of Ottoman sultans, was escorted into exile by British troops and his cousin Abdülmecid II (r. 1922-24) was installed as caliph.

The conference ended successfully for the Turks, and the Treaty of Lausanne, signed on 24 July 1923, granted recognition to all areas claimed by the National Pact, apart from Mosul in northern Iraq. Turkey was at last free to operate as an independent state, its only obligation to the past being the loans its sultans had incurred in the previous century. The Straits would remain under international control until 1936 but it was an astonishing turnaround.

Greece and Turkey arranged for a remarkable exchange of peoples. More than a million Greeks living in Turkey were sent to Greece and 400,000 Turks went the other way. Meanwhile, Mustafa Kemal – who would become known as 'Atatürk' (Father of the Turks) – began reshaping the Turkish state, basing his new model on the states of the west. In 1923, he broke with the past by transferring the capital from Istanbul to Ankara in the centre of Anatolia. A new constitution reaffirmed Turkey as a republic and all males aged 18 or more were given the vote. The president would be chosen by the assembly and it chose Atatürk who held the position until his death in 1938. There was only one party in the state – the Republican People's Party – and through this party Atatürk was able to exercise huge control over the legislature. He used this power to exorcise every aspect of the Ottomans from public life. In 1924, the caliphate was abolished by the National Assembly and all members of the Ottoman royal family were sent into exile.

Turkish nationalism concentrated on internal matters and there was a period of peace. By the time of Atatürk's death in 1938, he had stabilised his country. The transfer of power to his successor, his long-serving prime minister, Ismet Inonu (1884-1973), passed smoothly. Atatürk offended many, particularly those isolated from the urban centres, and his secularisation of Turkish society and his western tendencies antagonised many but the institutions he founded have endured. There could be no greater legacy than that.

Egyptian 'Independence'

In 1914, at the outbreak of war, Britain declared a Protectorate over Egypt, replacing the khedive, Abbas II, with his uncle Hussein Kamel who took the title of Sultan in December 1914. The grievances of the nationalists were exacerbated by the influx into Egypt of inexperienced and uncaring British officers and civil servants who treated the Egyptians like the inhabitants of an occupied country. Thousands of *fellahin* (peasants) were conscripted to fight in Palestine and their animals were requisitioned. There was wide-scale corruption involving conscription, and there were many other issues that created a very discontented population for whom self-determination seemed remote.

To the dismay of the Egyptian prime minister and the nationalists, Egypt was prevented by London from sending representatives to the Paris Peace Conference. This led to the resignation of the prime minister on 1 March 1919. Rioting and strikes broke out and the nationalist leaders were sent into exile in Malta. More unrest led to the Egyptian Revolution of 1919. It took the British army three weeks to restore order everywhere and many lost their lives. The new High Commissioner, Lord Allenby, adopted a conciliatory approach to the nationalists, freeing their exiled leaders. One of them, Saad Zaghloul (1859-1927), attended the conference but made little progress for his country. However, a commission set up under the Colonial Secretary Lord Milner (1854-1925) recommended that Egypt should become independent.

Milner explained to outraged imperialists that, 'Unless all our past declarations have been insincere... the establishment of Egypt as an independent state in intimate alliance with Britain is the goal to which all our efforts have been directed.' The Cabinet demurred, fearful that to be seen to give in to Egyptian nationalists, shortly after its recent accommodation with Sinn Fein in Ireland, would subject it to excoriation in the press. Finally, Viscount Allenby and the four principal British advisers to the Egyptian government threatened to resign and the Cabinet gave in. On 28 February 1922, Egypt was declared an independent sovereign state. Four points – known as the Four Reserved Points – were left to the discretion of Britain, however, although they remained to be agreed upon. These were the security of imperial communications; the defence of Egypt against foreign aggression or interference, direct or indirect; the protection of foreign residents and minorities; and the Sudan. Egypt was not allowed to join the League of Nations and Britain warned that organisation and any foreign power against intervention in Egyptian affairs.

The partial nature of Egyptian independence did not go unnoticed and some pointed out that it was less than the status of a British dominion, for example. The Egyptians grudgingly accepted their limited independence.

The Palestine Question

Britain had to be cognisant of the fact that Syria was France's special preserve. Since 1860, the French had expanded education there, had constructed railway lines and enjoyed many commercial concessions. There were those who believed that Palestine should be included in French interests in the region. The Sykes-Picot Agreement stipulated, however, that Palestine was to be governed by an international administration. Nothing was said about the Jews of whom there was still a small community in Palestine.

Napoleon, when he had invaded Palestine from Egypt in 1799, had proclaimed a manifesto in which he offered the Jews of the world 'the patrimony of Israel' while many nineteenth-century British Protestants believed that the restoration of the Jews to Palestine would represent the fulfillment of the Biblical scriptures.

Nothing much changed in the numbers of Jews in Palestine until 1881, however, when, following the assassination of Tsar Alexander II, there was anti-Jewish violence in Russia. Subsequent anti-Jewish legislation led to a mass exodus of Jews, many travelling to Britain and the United States but a number relocating to Palestine. By the First World War around 80,000 had settled there. This was not without opposition from Arabs. In the rest of Europe there was also a growing anti-Jewish feeling.

In 1896, Viennese journalist Theodor Herzl (1860-1904) produced a pamphlet entitled *The Jewish State*, proposing the creation of a Jewish state. It marked the birth of the Zionist movement. Herzl formed the World Zionist Organisation and, seven years later, the British government offered his organisation the opportunity to establish a Jewish settlement in British East Africa (roughly modern-day Kenya). Herzl was interested, but died before anything could happen. The prevailing view of Zionists from then on was that the Jewish state should be in Palestine.

During the war, the leaders of the Zionist movement were living in Britain and the United States. Dr. Chaim Weizmann (1874-1952) was a chemistry lecturer at Manchester University and Louis D. Brandeis (1856-1941) was a Supreme Court Justice. The British Foreign Secretary, Arthur Balfour, was a convert to Zionism and President Woodrow Wilson (1856-1924) was 'warmly responsive to the Zionist ideal'. In such circumstances and after a great deal of debate amongst Zionists around the world, a proposal was made to the British government in 1917 calling for 'recognition of Palestine as a National Home for the Jewish people'. After the more uncompromising elements of the submission were removed, the document was approved and appeared in November 1917. The original submission by the Zionists had been forthright and uncompromising, calling for internal autonomy for a Jewish state in Palestine, freedom of immigration and the setting up of a Jewish National Colonising Corporation to deal with the resettlement of the new country. But the Balfour Declaration was ambiguous and hesitant. Why was it made at all? It was purely pragmatic, as British Prime Minister Lloyd George (1863-1945) later explained:

> '...it was believed that Jewish sympathy or the reverse would make a substantial difference one way or another to the Allied cause. In particular Jewish sympathy would confirm the support of American Jewry, and would make it more difficult for Germany to reduce her military commitments and improve her economic position on the eastern front. The Zionist leaders gave us a definite promise that, if the Allies committed themselves to giving facilities for the establishment of a national home for the Jews in Palestine, they would do their best to rally Jewish sentiment and support throughout the world to the Allied cause. They kept their word.'

Around 90 per cent of the Palestinian population was non-Jewish. British army officials were keen, therefore, to keep knowledge of the Balfour Declaration from them. But, in reality, the aspirations of the Arabs were irrelevant to politicians such as Woodrow Wilson, Arthur Balfour and Lloyd George. They were being treated in the same way as Native Americans in the United States and the Bantu in Africa. The Zionist objective was clear, as Dr. Weizmann unequivocally stated at the Peace Conference:

'To make Palestine as Jewish as England is English or America American.'

The Zionists ascribed no credibility to the Arab nationalists and made efforts to divide them. This was shown to have failed in 1936 when the Arabs launched a rebellion that continued for the following three years. The Jews realised it was pointless trying to divide the Arabs and began dealing with them as a whole, but were adamant that nothing could deflect them from their goal. In 1946, the *Palestine Post* reported that the Zionist Labour party, Mapai, the most powerful Jewish party in Palestine, had passed a resolution that appealed to the Arab people and assured them that the Jewish people were 'ready to cooperate as equals for the peaceful development of Palestine'. At the same time, 'all measures intended to destroy the Zionist programme would be fought'. Dr. Chaim Weizmann had contended that he was engaged in a policy of 'stretching out his hands to the Arabs in friendship', but Mapai's uncompromising statement contrasted greatly with this.

While moderate Zionists were critical of the Palestine authorities for not suppressing the more extreme Arab elements, hardline Zionists theorised that the trouble between Arab and Jew was a British creation. They also believed the British to have more sympathy for the Arab cause than the Zionist one. In fact, British policy diverged from Zionist aims from 1939 and significantly so from 1945. Nonetheless, a clash between the two sides seemed inevitable from the outset and the first Arab riots against the Mandate occurred in 1920, the Zionists accusing the British of being slow to disperse the troublemakers. Prime Minister Lloyd George responded by replacing the military administration of Palestine with a civil authority. The Mandate provided its charter and its first High Commissioner was Sir Herbert Samuel (1870-1963). Samuel, although not religious, had been born a Jew and was, therefore, the first Jew in two thousand years to govern the historic land of Israel. The Arabs, of course, suspected him of Zionist sympathies. Samuel, however, was fairly even-handed in his dealings with each side and eventually, he would even be criticised by extreme Zionists for being pro-Arab. But with the unrest continuing, the British Cabinet decided to clarify its policy. The Churchill White Paper of 1922 emphasised that the UK government had never contemplated 'the disappearance or the subordination of the Arabic population, language or culture in Palestine'. It also stated that 'the terms of the (Balfour) Declaration... do not contemplate that Palestine as a whole should be converted into a Jewish National Home, but that such a home should be founded *in Palestine*'. The White Paper was notable for acknowledging for the first time the rights of the Arab population of Palestine. Nonetheless, the Legislative Council it proposed was boycotted by the Arabs who still refused to acknowledge the legitimacy of the Mandate.

By 1928, the Jewish population numbered 150,000, or around 16 per cent of the entire Palestinian population. Although Jewish farming initiatives were successful, life was still difficult. There was a distinct lack of public funds to help them and unemployment became a major problem. Things were so bad that in 1927 more Jews began to leave Palestine than came in. Meanwhile, the Arab population began to increase as a result of a high birth rate, the end of Ottoman conscription, and the lowering of the death rate due to better public health initiatives and illegal immigration. The 1937 Royal Commission Report succinctly summed up the prevailing situation: '...a conflict had been created between two national ideals, and under the system imposed by the Mandate it could only be solved if one of these ideals were abandoned.'

Transjordan

The 1920 San Remo Conference, with the leaders of Britain, France, Italy and Japan in attendance, determined that the Transjordan region should be allotted to Britain, as part of the Palestinian Mandate. When the French took over Syria in July 1920, High Commissioner Samuel convened a conference of the local Arab notables of the Transjordan area and told them that the British government was prepared to allow them self-determination. Before a system of government could be introduced, however, the Amir Abdullah announced that he would be leading a rebellion against the French in Syria. Advancing to Amman, he was not challenged by the British and took control of the region. The British agreed to recognise him as ruler of Transjordan on condition that he backed down from his activities against the French and accepted help from Britain in establishing a modern system of government. Britain then succeeded in having Transjordan excluded from the conditions of the Mandate for Palestine, including those that dealt with Jewish immigration and the establishment of a Jewish National Home. In 1923, the British recognised Abdullah's government on condition that it was constitutional.

Abdullah would abide by the conditions of his rule and he would obtain the independence of his country and the position of monarch in 1946. It would become known as the Hashemite Kingdom of the Jordan. He continued to accept financial help from the British which did not endear him to Arabs who were also suspicious of his expansionist aspirations. He envisaged a Greater Syria that would incorporate Transjordan, Syria, Lebanon and Palestine, ruled from Damascus. It was for these reasons that Abdullah was assassinated in July 1951, shot dead by a Palestinian from the Husseini clan. The former prime minister of Lebanon,

Riad Bey Al Solh had been assassinated four days previously and it was said that the two deaths were linked to rumours that both Lebanon and Jordan were negotiating a peace agreement with Israel following the Arab-Israeli War of 1948.

Egyptian 'Democracy' (1924-36)

A constitution was proclaimed in Egypt in 1923 and elections to its first parliament were staged the following January. The Wafd Party took 90 per cent of the seats, and Saad Zaghloul became the country's first prime minister. The constitution, however, gave the king extensive powers, such as the right to appoint the prime minister and to dissolve parliament which made it an inherently weak institution. King Fuad I (r. 1922-36), for instance, was in the habit of dismissing governments as and when he wanted. Furthermore, the British still interfered, further inhibiting the credibility of the Egyptian parliamentary system. It was also damaged by the dictatorial manner of Zaghloul, who was every bit as authoritarian as the king. He held the opposition in disdain and the civil service was filled with Wafdist supporters regardless of whether they were qualified for the jobs. While the Wafd Party, the king and the British jostled for position, the Four Reserved Points hovered all the time in the background. Meanwhile, governments did not last long and were interspersed with periods of royal rule. The great issues that dogged the country at the time were not being dealt with as competing factions vied for power.

In 1936, increasingly, concerned by Fascist Italy's seizure of Ethiopia, the British agreed to a renegotiation of the 1922 declaration of independence. A treaty was signed by which Britain recognised Egypt's independence but British troops were to remain in the Suez Canal zone and Britain's right to defend Egypt if it was attacked was reasserted. One of the conditions stated that Egyptian troops, officials and immigrants were once again to be admitted to the Sudan, but it stipulated that the Sudanese government would appoint British or Egyptian officials only if a suitable Sudanese candidate could not be found. For the first time Sudanese self-determination was acknowledged. The only real difference to the 1922 declaration, however, was that this time it was signed by an Egyptian Wafdist government. Thus, Egyptian consent was being given formally for the British occupation of the Suez Canal zone. In 1937, the Montreux Convention at last abolished the Capitulations and allowed for the abolition of the Mixed Courts by 1949.

King Fuad was succeeded by his son, Farouk (r. 1936-52), but neither this, nor the greater degree of independence, changed things. Farouk was initially popular, but soon became disliked because of his self-indulgent lifestyle. Furthermore, the ruling elite was becoming increasingly remote from the people it ruled. Leadership was poor, especially after Zaghloul's death in 1927, and corruption was rife. The population was dismayed by their rulers' insistence on European ways and the imposition of these on the nation. Those at the top maintained that European society was innately superior to Egyptian society and traditional beliefs were constantly under attack. This rejection in the 1930s by the intellectual elite of Egypt's traditions and the subsequent drive towards secularism led ordinary people to seek organisations that were associated with Islamic activism. The most important of these was the Society of Muslim Brothers, more commonly known as the Muslim Brotherhood.

Founded in 1928 by schoolteacher Hasan al-Banna (1906-49), the Muslim Brotherhood was involved in political activism as well as Islamic charity work. Its stated aim was to use the Koran and Sunnah as the 'sole reference point for... ordering the life of the Muslim family, individual community... and state'. By the close of the 1930s, it had 500 branches in Egypt and its membership numbered in the thousands. Al-Banna called for the restoration of the *Shariah* but wanted it to be compatible with the requirements of a modern society. While politicians fought amongst themselves, the Muslim Brotherhood was active in the community, al-Banna calling for land redistribution, social welfare programmes and local, instead of foreign, investment. The Brotherhood allied with Egypt's emerging labour movement and demanded rights for workers. It also set up initiatives in the weaving, transport and construction industries, giving employees shares. It founded schools that combined religious instruction with more general education, it opened free medical clinics and, when the Depression hit Egypt, soup kitchens run by the Brotherhood fed the urban poor. Understandably, the Muslim Brotherhood was embraced by those in need as well as by students and the young, attracted by its uncompromising rejection of the 1936 agreement with the British. The Brotherhood would emerge from the Second World War as a dominant force in Egyptian life.

Iraq Between the Wars

Under the Ottoman Empire, Mesopotamia had been split into three disparate provinces. The northern region of Mosul had economic links with neighbouring Anatolia and Greater Syria; the central province of Baghdad was agricultural and enjoyed trading links with Iran and the southwest; and the southern region of Basra looked towards the Persian Gulf and trade onwards from there with India. Under the British Mandate of 1920, these three states somewhat arbitrarily became Iraq. This created obstacles to building a nation.

The population was 80 per cent Arab, slightly more than half of which were Shiites linked to Iran's *ulama*. The rest of the Arabic population was Sunni to whom the British gave their political backing, helping them to become prominent in the new state's political life. Meanwhile, around 20 per cent of the population were Kurds who lived mostly in the north of the country. The Kurds regarded northern Iraq – and parts of Turkey, Syria and Iran – as their homeland and were a distinct people with their own language and culture. To this day, they refuse to be assimilated into Iraq, a source of ongoing discord. There was considerable potential for further religious and ethnic tensions with the existence of the Assyrian Christian minority and the large Jewish enclave in Baghdad. Large areas of the country, outside the cities, had been virtually ignored by the Ottomans, leaving them to be controlled by tribal confederations unused to interference from the centre. A 1920 uprising by the tribes of the Euphrates lasted several months and gave the British an indication of the difficulties they would encounter in imposing control. As the first manifestation of Iraq's desire to be free of foreign rule, it represented an important moment in the nation's history. The rebellion was brought under control but at great cost – around 10,000 Iraqis and 450 British troops lost their lives.

The financial cost was staggering and convinced the British government that the issue was how to maintain the security of the route to India and the Iraqi and Iranian oil facilities without having to spend fortunes on directly governing an unwilling population. The answer was to use treaties and to give more responsibility to the Iraqi government. They sought a ruler who would be acceptable to the Iraqis but would also be able to work with them, choosing the man who had led the Arab Revolt – Amir Faisal, son of Sharif Hussein. Elected king in a carefully controlled referendum, Faisal was crowned in 1921. Iraq became a hereditary constitutional monarchy with an elected bicameral legislature. An Iraqi army was created, limited initially by the British to 7,500 men.

The influential Lord Curzon was disappointed: 'This is not an Arab government inspired and helped by British advice, but a British government infused with Arab elements.' It only helped to foment more nationalist irritation and defiance. As did the increased taxation – three-and-a-half times what it had been under the Ottomans in 1911 – which fell most heavily on the *fellahin*. But the landlords, the elite and the tribes, who had previously managed to escape paying tax altogether, were also hit hard. Of course, the Iraqis had no say in how the revenues were spent and a great deal went into administration and paying for the huge number of British personnel.

Faisal reigned until 1933, during which time Iraq had 15 governments; a further 21 would follow in the next four years. The members were always drawn from the same wealthy, educated elite and Iraq was still a long way from democracy. In 1932, when the country became independent, political parties were abolished in the name of 'national unity' and were not permitted again until 1946. Furthermore, most of the men who were prominent in Iraqi political circles were Sunni Muslims, even though Shiites made up a majority of the population. In fact, Shiites would remain excluded from political life in Iraq until the United States and its allies invaded the country in 2003.

Faisal had initially withdrawn from matters of state when the constitution was introduced, but he was soon interfering again, advised by British officials. Only ministers of whom he approved could be appointed but he was, in reality, used by the British to maintain their control over the country. He did do some good, however, supporting the settlement of the tribes and ensuring that some of the country's oil revenue was allocated to development projects, and it is probable that without him Iraq's independence would have been subject to delay. When he died in 1933, he was succeeded by his incompetent 21-year-old son, Ghazi (r.1933-39). Soon the government was in chaos, cabinets coming and going at the rate of five a year between 1932 and 1936. That year, Bakr Sidqi (1890-1937), an Iraqi general who had ruthlessly crushed an Assyrian uprising in 1933, staged probably the Arab world's first modern military coup when he succeeded in having the corrupt government of Yasin al-Hashimi (1882-1937) removed from power. Sidqi became military dictator but there was little change and, after he was assassinated in 1937, things returned to normal with governments made up of the same old faces.

Iran's Last Dynasty

At the end of the First World War, thousands of British troops were based in Iran. The Iranian government was terrified of the new Communist threat and feared an invasion which gave the British government the opportunity to become involved in the affairs of the country, offering protection in exchange for certain rights. With the Anglo-Persian Agreement of 1919 Britain obtained the right to decide Iranian trade tariffs and gained influence over government appointments and the Iranian army.

The Persian Cossack Brigade was an elite cavalry unit in the Iranian army. Modelled on the Caucasian Cossack regiments of the Russian army, the brigade was commanded by Russian officers, its troops ethnic Caucasians and Persians. They sometimes exercised political power and were pivotal in the Revolution of 1905-11. They would play a part in the rise of the last Persian dynasty, founded by one of their own, Reza Pahlavi (r. 1925-41).

By 1921, Iran was in turmoil. The ruling Qajar dynasty was corrupt and inefficient and, although oil-rich, Iran relied heavily on Britain and Russia for economic and military aid. The Cossack Brigade was the only regular military force that the weak and incompetent Shah Ahmad (r. 1909-25) had at his command. The British were despondent about the ability of the country's leaders to rule properly but were engaged in a power struggle with the Russians for control of this vital Middle Eastern country.

On 18 February that year, Reza Pahlavi, commander of the Tabriz battalion of the Persian Cossacks, 'led his troops into Teheran and forced the government to resign, making himself minister of war and forcing the shah to appoint the equally pro-British Zia'eddin Tabatabaee (1888-1969) prime minister. Tabatabaee lasted until 25 May when he was replaced by Ahmad Qavam (1876-1955). By 1923, Pahlavi was himself prime minister and two years later the Iranian parliament deposed the Qajar dynasty and declared Reza Pahlavi shah. In just five years he had risen from an officer in the army to Shah of Iran. He proclaimed his desire to make Iran a modern, secular kingdom.

The new monarch's first objective was to reduce the hold that Britain had on his country. To that end, he signed a treaty of friendship with the Soviet Union by which the Russians gave up a number of their facilities in Iran, including railways and ports. With the Soviet threat removed, the new shah reasoned, Iran no longer needed British protection. The end of Russian support for separatist groups in Iran allowed him to come down heavily on the movements' leaders. He rescinded the Anglo-Persian Agreement of 1919, which had never been ratified by the Iranian parliament anyway, and imposed protective trade tariffs on Britain that were designed to promote growth in Persian industries. He imposed a new tax on the Anglo-Persian Oil Company that had been established to provide Britain with most of the profits, only a small percentage coming to Iran. When APOC refused to pay the tax, Reza removed its oil development rights. The British rushed to the negotiating table and a deal more favourable to Iran was concluded.

Domestically, he embarked on a plan for the modernisation of the country and finance was ploughed into Iran's ancient and outmoded infrastructure. Roads, railways, bridges and power plants were constructed. But it was in the area of religion that he came up against his biggest hurdles. He believed Islam to be an impediment to economic development. *Shariah* courts were abolished, removing the power of the Muslim clerics to control civil and criminal cases. Clerics also controlled education in the country with religious schools. Therefore, the shah established a public school system. In a bid to stamp out radicalism, he intervened in the way in which mullahs were selected. They would henceforth have to sit a series of examinations set by the government. He forced universities to accept female students, further outraging the mullahs, and girls were encouraged to attend his public schools. He even outlawed the veil. His regime, however, was autocratic. Trade unions, communism and political dissent of any type were stamped upon. An extensive network of secret police operated, meaning that no one was safe, and he also tried to control the Iranian parliament, putting the army in charge of it to negate opposition.

When the Second World War broke out, the shah was in a tricky position. He had cultivated close ties with Germany, partly to hinder the imperial aspirations of Britain and Russia but also because he openly admired Adolf Hitler and the Nazis, and believed that, as had happened with his treaty with the USSR, his closeness to Germany would make Iran more independent of Britain. Iran declared neutrality at the start of the war but the country was of huge strategic importance to Britain. The British government feared that the Abadan Oil Refinery, owned by the Anglo-Iranian Oil Company (AIOC), would be seized by the

Germans. Furthermore, following the invasion of Russia by the Nazis in June 1941, one of the main routes for transporting much-needed supplies to the Soviets was via the 'Persian Corridor' through which travelled the Trans-Iranian Railway. Pressure by the British and the Russians on the shah was to no avail, only stirring up anti-British demonstrations in Teheran. After the shah had refused to expel German nationals a surprise Allied invasion was launched in August 1941. The Allies took control of Iran and the shah was forced to abdicate in favour of his son, Mohammad Reza Pahlavi (1919-80). Reza Shah was sent into exile and died three years later in South Africa.

Syria Between the Wars

Greater Syria suffered greatly during the First World War, around 18 per cent of its population losing their lives. Syrian lives were further disrupted by the imposition of French rule after the war. The French claimed to be acting to protect Christian communities in the Levant, amongst whom were the Catholic Maronites of Mount Lebanon. Of course, this religious aspect to French hegemony only served to increase the hatred of Muslims for the French. France claimed to have a stake in the region, having invested heavily in the infrastructure and in commerce during the last years of Ottoman rule. They were also, of course, in competition with Britain in the Middle East and there were those in France who believed that the country could never be considered a real power in the Mediterranean unless it had a possession in the Levant. Thus, they undertook a military operation to end Faisal's brief reign and obtained the permission of the League of Nations for a Mandate.

The French guarded their power jealously in Syria, neglecting to prepare the country for independence as the Mandate demanded, and encouraging discord between the various religious, ethnic and regional groupings within the country so that no one group could take power. They began by creating Greater Lebanon in 1920, adding the coastal cities of Beirut, Sidon, Tyre and Tripoli to Mount Lebanon. The fertile Beqaa Valley was transferred from Syria into Lebanon to the benefit of the Maronite Christians, the largest religious grouping within the newly expanded Lebanon. The areas moved into Lebanon, apart from Beirut, were largely Muslim and these people objected to becoming part of a region dominated by Christians.

To further impede the development of a cultural and national identity for Syria, France divided it into political units. In 1922 the two minority groups, the Alawites and the Druze, were each given a separate state. They would remain separate from Syria until 1942. In 1924, Damascus and Aleppo were amalgamated into the State of Syria which also contained the large cities of Homs and Hama. Thus, the Alawites and Druze were cut off from the nation's politics, and the French ensured that Syrian political life would be dominated by the wealthy and conservative Sunni Muslims of the cities. This would create great problems in the future.

On the whole, the local people were unable to gain political and administrative experience. The French occupied all the important positions in the government bureaucracy, and where Syrians held positions of responsibility, a French official always retained the veto over their decisions. One way for social and religious groups other than the Sunni elite to become upwardly mobile was by joining the army's officer corps. The Sunnis looked upon the idea of a military career with disdain, thus leaving the way open to others, and when Syria finally gained independence in 1946, the army, populated with officers from minority groups, challenged the Sunni dominance of Syrian political life.

Resistance to the French Mandate erupted into full-blown rebellion in July 1925. In October, the French subjected Damascus to a two-day aerial and artillery bombardment that took the lives of around 1,400 civilians and it was only in 1927, following the arrival of huge contingents of reinforcements, that they were able to subdue the rebels. Although 6,000 Syrians and many of their own troops died and the financial cost was huge, the French would not be diverted from their plans for the control of Syria.

Syrian leaders formed the National Bloc, an organisation that would become the focus of independence aspirations throughout the rest of the Mandate. Its founders were from the region's Ottoman past who had done well then and operated in the same way now. They espoused the anti-French feelings of the urban Syrians but at the same time they had to adopt a policy of cooperation with the French, convincing them that they could manage the aspirations of the people. They were naturally conservative and really sought to preserve the status quo and, therefore, their wealth and power. Seeing them as intermediaries with those they were governing, the French decided to work with them to avoid problems such as the ones they had experienced from 1925 to 1927.

In 1929, a constitution was drawn up by an elected assembly but the French rejected it, imposing their own version the following year. It simply reasserted the Mandate and, for the next six years, the decisions of Syrian prime ministers, presidents and legislature were rendered futile by the French power of veto on all legislation. In 1936, however, when Léon Blum (1872-1950) came to power in France at the head of a Popular Front coalition, it was hoped that things might change. At first, all seemed to be going well and a treaty was drafted that would have seen Syria admitted to the League of Nations, the key to independence. But in 1937, Blum's coalition fell apart and the French parliament refused to ratify the treaty. In 1939, the French High Commissioner suspended the Syrian constitution and dissolved parliament. He also made the Alawite and Druze states independent once again and upset the Syrians even more by handing the Alexandretta region (modern-day Iskenderun) over to Turkey. The National Bloc was seriously discredited by its lack of success and the Mandate remained firmly in place after twenty years. Syria was a long way, it seemed, from independence and the French were contributing to a terrible legacy of political instability in the country.

Lebanon

Greater Lebanon was created by the French with the sole purpose of ensuring that the Maronite Christians did not end up in a Syrian Muslim state. Thus, in Lebanon they were the single biggest religious grouping although they only represented about 30 per cent of the entire population of the new state. The Christians, naturally, tended to want to turn their backs on the Arab world and look more towards France and Europe, while the Sunni Muslims thought otherwise. It was a volatile situation exacerbated by the geographical spread of the various religious communities across the country. Added to this was the religious diversity of the local notables who worked on behalf of their clients – sharing the same religion – and against other religious groups. These opposing interests made governing Lebanon particularly difficult.

Nonetheless, because it was more accommodating to the Mandate than Syria, on account of its Francophile Maronite community, the path to independence was much easier. A Lebanese republic was created in 1926 with a constitution that offered a single chamber of deputies based on religious representation and a president elected by the chamber. He had wide-ranging powers including that of choosing the prime minister and the cabinet. The Mandate remained in place, however, and foreign and military matters remained in French hands, the High Commissioner retaining the right to suspend parliament and the constitution. This right was exercised on two occasions – between 1932 and 1934 and in 1939. French advisers continued to exercise a great deal of authority even over domestic matters.

In 1936, France and Lebanon agreed a treaty similar to the one France had signed with Syria that same year. It guaranteed 'the fair representation of all the country's sects in the government and high administration'. Maronite politician Émile Eddé (1883-1949) was elected president but adroitly selected a Muslim, Khayr al-Din al-Ahdab (1894-1941), as prime minister. It was the beginning of a custom in Lebanese politics that lasted until the late 1980s – the president would be a Maronite Christian and the prime minister would be a Sunni Muslim. It was an act that finally reconciled Muslims to the notion of a greater Syria and, although tensions remained, it showed how this nation of such religious diversity could be governed. But independence still did not arrive. The 1936 treaty was not ratified by the French parliament and, come the Second World War, the High Commissioner suspended the constitution and dissolved parliament once again.

The Second World War

1939-1941

The Middle East became a very important theatre of war during the conflict of 1939 to 1945. Turkey remained neutral, but the new states moulded from the demise of the Ottoman Empire, although non-belligerent, were occupied by participants in the war – Great Britain and France – and were, therefore, involved. The British had similar objectives in the region as they had during the First World War – the retention of India and the safeguarding of the oil facilities in Iran. All seemed well until Italy entered the war on the German side in July 1940. British troops faced Italian forces in Libya and there were Italian garrisons in Eritrea. Egypt was bombed by Italian planes and it seemed likely that the Italians would launch a full-scale invasion of that country. Commonwealth troops from South Africa, New Zealand and Australia were sent in to bolster the British forces.

In September 1940, as expected, the Italians invaded Egypt, making it as far as Sidi Barrani about 59 miles beyond the Libyan border, but the British drove them back to Libya by the end of that year. Reinforced, however, by German troops led by the indomitable General Erwin Rommel (1891-1944), 'the Desert Fox', the Axis powers advanced into Egypt in April the following year. After Crete was captured that same month, the British hold over the Eastern Mediterranean was in danger.

Meanwhile, in Iraq, nationalist German sympathisers seized power in March 1941, and Rashid Ali al-Gaylani (1892-1965) became prime minister. His government failed to respond to a request by the British government to move troops across Iraq, contravening the Anglo-Iraqi Treaty, and this meant that the two countries were at war with one another. The Axis forces promised to Iraq were insufficient and arrived late and, with an Indian force landing at Basra, the revolt collapsed. Rashid Ali and his government fled the country.

Syria and Lebanon, meanwhile, fell into the hands of the Vichy government after the fall of France in June 1940. Britain announced that it would not permit the occupation of these countries by the Germans, and when German planes landed at Syrian airfields, en route to help Rashid Ali's short-lived Iraqi government, the British and the Free French launched an invasion from Palestinian bases. After six weeks' fighting, the Vichy troops were defeated and an armistice was signed.

1942

Japanese victories in the Far East forced the British to send tanks there from the Middle East, leaving the way clear for Rommel to advance towards Egypt. There was an ambivalent feeling towards the war in Egypt, many believing it had nothing to do with them. German property was seized and German nationals were interned, but there were many in the government who leaned towards the Axis powers. The British High Commissioner persuaded the Egyptian King Farouk to replace dissenters – especially the prime minister, Ali Mahir (1882-1960) – and the king complied, providing minsters more sympathetic to the

Allies. Many in Egypt still believed the country should remain neutral, however. Others, such as General Aziz al-Misri (1879-1965), the Egyptian chief-of-staff, and a young captain, Anwar Sadat (1918-81), a future president of Egypt, supported the Axis powers. British Prime Minister Winston Churchill had no time for Egyptian nationalist feelings and, aware that the Egyptian army had little stomach for the war, ordered it to be moved from the Western Desert to the Nile Delta.

While King Farouk was absent from Cairo a new crisis developed when the British government forced the Egyptian government to sever relations with the Vichy regime. Incensed, Farouk forced his prime minister to resign, reintroducing the pro-Axis Ali Mahir to the cabinet. The British Ambassador, Miles Lampson (1880-1964), was keen to see a Wafdist government installed, aware that it would provide support for the Allied cause but he was also aware that Farouk opposed this idea. Eventually, Lampson delivered an ultimatum to the king and, when no response was received by the deadline, British troops surrounded the Abdeen Palace in Cairo. Rather than abdicate, Farouk gave in and Wafd politician Mustafa al-Nahhas (1879-1965) was asked to form a government. Nationalists viewed the monarch's capitulation as a humiliation for Egypt and it laid the foundations for the 1952 Revolution.

The sympathy for the Axis powers was, indeed, strange. After all, the Nazis viewed the Arabs as racially inferior and the persecution of the Jews in Europe had increased Jewish migration to Palestine. While the Nazis had continued to encourage Jewish migration, Britain had attempted to place limits on it, in the hope of gaining the goodwill of the Arabs. Still, many Arabs sided with the Germans and the Axis powers exploited this with propaganda that influenced many younger Arab thinkers and politicians. Of course, one reason for Arab support was the feeling at the start of the war, before the entry of America, that the Axis nations would be victorious. Arabs also considered the Axis to be the enemy of the West and any such enemy was the Arabs' friend.

The main role played by the Middle East in the war was in the provision of resources and facilities. The Nazis had no real interest in the region, focused as they were on Europe. But, at the end of the war, Allied troops remained in many of the countries of the Middle East, despite promises of independence and withdrawal of their forces. Some of these nations were, of course, under British colonial control, but others were ruled by leaders who were hated by their peoples because they seemed to be nothing more than Allied puppets. At the same time, however, they never quite gained the complete trust of the Allies.

The Modern Middle East

Nationalist Aspirations and Oil

The Axis and the Allied powers had both encouraged the nationalist aspirations of the countries of the Middle East. Some Arab states had gained a degree of independence and were making their way in the world. The Arab League was founded in March 1945 with six members – Egypt, Iraq, Transjordan, Lebanon, Saudi Arabia and Syria. Its objective was to 'draw closer the relations between member States and co-ordinate collaboration between them, to safeguard their independence and sovereignty, and to consider in a general way the affairs and interests of the Arab countries'.

The first oil-drilling in the Middle East took place in the Russian-controlled parts of the region in 1842, in the Absheron peninsula in Azerbaijan. The first refinery was constructed at Baku in 1863 and within fifteen years a pipeline linked Baku with the refinery. The Baku oil fields were supplying Russia with about 95 per cent of all her oil needs by the end of the First World War. Meanwhile, European and American businessmen were agitating for concessions in the Iranian and Ottoman territories. As we have seen, the first major concession was granted by the Shah of Iran, Mozaffar ad-Din, to the Englishman William Knox D'Arcy. For £20,000 D'Arcy was given a 60-year concession to explore for oil in an area of 480,000 square miles and the Iranian government was to receive 16 per cent of the company's annual profits. It was an agreement that the Iranians would regret until the late twentieth century. This was just the first of many such deals by which British, Dutch, French or American companies would exploit Middle Eastern oil. Oilfields were opened in Iraq, Arabia and elsewhere, as the Middle East became one the world's major oil-producing areas. This would lead at last to development. Better communications were necessary and new roads were built; printing, newspapers, cinema, radio and the paraphernalia of modern life soon arrived in the region, coupled with economic development.

The British and the French had been interested in the region because of its strategic importance. It had acted as an effective buffer zone, helping the British to protect their great imperial possession, India, and the French to safeguard their North African colonies. The French had also claimed to have cultural reasons for their presence in the Middle East – the protection of the Christian minorities in the region, especially the Catholics, and the dissemination of French culture. Economic considerations had not been high on the agenda until the discovery of oil, although it was not as important in the early twentieth century as it became in the late twentieth and early twenty-first centuries.

Ultimately, however, it is not in doubt that the people of the Middle East were better off in 1939 than they had been in 1914. With British and French involvement in the region most of them enjoyed a higher standard of living; they had better amenities and could expect to live longer. There were more services and their countries had better infrastructures. There were other benefits, such as language – the use of English and French brought many people of the Middle East into the modern world. It also brought modern scientific and cultural ideas to them more easily.

Naturally, however, there were those who saw the influence of Western culture as an evil to be abhorred.

Independence and Uprisings

The post-war period brought chaos to the world, with millions of people being displaced and the Soviet Union making advances in Central and Eastern Europe. In Asia and Africa serious questions were posed by the retreat of the imperial powers. Although its problems were not as great, the Middle East was not immune and there were frequent upheavals. These were often more intense and less open to political or diplomatic solutions.

As in other colonies of the imperial powers around the world, what was uppermost in everyone's mind was independence. Turkey, Afghanistan and Iran had long been free of the imperial yoke and the years between the wars had added several more to the list of independent states — Egypt, Iraq, Saudi Arabia and Yemen, although the first two of these countries had not fully shaken off the shackles of their imperial rulers, bound as they were by unequal treaties and the presence of British troops and bases on their soil.

Meanwhile, Syria became a sovereign state when it was liberated from Vichy control in 1941 and gained full independence from the French Mandate in October 1945. British troops entered Lebanon in 1941, the British government fearful that the Germans would seize control. That year the French announced that the country would become independent and elections were held in 1943. At the end of the war, the Mandate was ended and Lebanon was admitted to the newly formed United Nations. Transjordan gained independence in March 1946. By the early 1950s, the European powers had withdrawn completely from the region.

Other Arab countries soon followed those already independent – Libya in 1951; Sudan, Tunisia and Morocco in 1956; Mauritania in 1960; Kuwait in 1961; Algeria in 1962; South Yemen (formerly Aden) in 1967; and the Gulf states in 1971. Most achieved independence through negotiation but two – Algeria and South Yemen – got there only after a long and bitter struggle.

Even with the creation of these new states, however, the old problems and conflicts did not go away and, in fact, some new ones emerged. A state such as Saudi Arabia had advantages in that, although its population was made up of different tribal and regional groups, it was at least all Arab and all Muslim and, apart from areas in the east of the new country, it was all Sunni. The other states had internal rivalries and age-old enmities within their borders. This led to civil war, rebellion and revolution.

The Lebanon was one of the worst, riven with internal divisions driven by rival factions and sometimes there were yet further conflicts within these factions. Civil war ripped the country apart in 1958, between 1975 and 1976, and between 1983 and 1991. Similarly, southern Arabia was also in constant turmoil. With the support of Egypt, a republic was created there in 1962, but in North Yeman there was conflict for a number of years, between Saudi and Egyptian forces and between the royalists and the republicans. Another civil war erupted in the united Yemen in 1990. Between 1965 and 1975, Yemen was also embroiled in the conflict in Dhofar which was trying to secede from the Sultanate of Oman. It took an Iranian expeditionary force to quell the uprising. Meanwhile, force was used elsewhere to subdue uprisings. Turkey and Iraq both used troops to deal with unrest amongst their Kurdish minorities, and Iraq sent in its army against the Shiites who populated its central and southern regions, despite the fact that they actually represented a majority in the country. In the Sudan, there was perpetual conflict between the Arabic-speaking

Muslim north and the non-Arab, non-Muslim Africans who lived in the south of the country. In 1970, Jordan also experienced difficulties, when the Palestine Liberation Organisation rebelled against the state but were defeated. Algeria, too, was convulsed by a bloody civil war in the early 1990s in which around 100,000 people lost their lives.

Post-War Palestine

The Jewish Agency had done all it could during the war to ingratiate itself with the British. It provided hospitality for troops on leave and disseminated propaganda designed to persuade them of the success of the Jewish National Home and to convince them that the Jews in Palestine could get on with the Arabs when the latter were not being encouraged to act against them by their leaders and the British. The collective settlements – kibbutzim – and the contribution to daily life made by the trade union organisation Histadrut were particularly impressive to those of a socialist tendency. Thus, when a Labour government was elected in Great Britain in July 1945, the Zionists were excited. After all, this was the party that only a few months previously had declared itself in favour of unlimited migration of Jews to Palestine. But little changed and the Zionists began to become agitated. The Jewish Agency was at the time collaborating with Jewish terrorist groups such as the Stern Group and the Irgun, even though they officially denounced them, and it was proposed by one member of the Agency that they cause 'one serious incident' that would serve as a warning to the British. On the night of 31 October, one of the terrorist groups, the Palmach, blew up railway lines in 153 places in Palestine and also destroyed three police boats that were used to prevent the arrival of illegal immigrants. There was an attempt by the Stern Group to blow up the oil refinery at Haifa and the Irgun attacked railway yards. The British government, meanwhile, had come under pressure from the American President Harry S. Truman (1884-1972) to open the doors to around 100,000 displaced European Jews and this could not be ignored. A Committee of Enquiry was established 'to examine the position of Jews in those countries in Europe where they have been victims of Nazi persecution... and the political, economic and social condition in Palestine as they bear upon the problem of Jewish immigration and settlement therein, and the well-being of the peoples now living therein'.

The Zionists were incensed and held a strike in protest. Government buildings were set on fire in Jerusalem and the Jewish Agency issued a strong statement:

'The policy to which the British government pledged itself in the Balfour Declaration and the Mandate sprang from the recognition that the Jewish problem can be effectively solved only by the greatest possible concentration of Jews in Palestine and by the restoration of Jewish nationhood... The Jewish Agency... upholds the right of every Jew impelled by material or spiritual urge to settle in Palestine... The Jewish people... will spare no effort or sacrifice until the restoration of the Jewish Commonwealth of Palestine has been achieved.'

A few weeks later, the Criminal Investigation Department (CID) headquarters in Jerusalem was blown up by the Irgun, killing seven police officers and soldiers. Two more died in further attacks in Jaffa and Tel Aviv. The Agency dissociated itself from these acts, denouncing them for the loss of life but added that, while Britain pursued its current policy, they could do nothing to prevent them. Against this background, the Committee of Enquiry released its report in which it failed to come to a clear conclusion, recommending the continuation of the Mandate 'until the hostility between Jews and Arabs disappears'. The 100,000 Jewish victims of persecution were to be granted admission to Palestine 'while ensuring that the rights and position of other sections of the population were not prejudiced'. It went on to emphasise that violence should be suppressed: '… we express the view that the Jewish Agency should at once resume active cooperation with the Mandatory in the suppression of terrorism and illegal immigration, and in the maintenance of law and order'. Before the immigrants were allowed to enter Palestine it was imperative that the British persuaded the Jewish Agency to actively work for the suppression of terrorism. The Arabs were furious with this change to the 1939 White Paper and demanded the end of the Mandate, the withdrawal of British troops and the creation of an Arab state. They threatened that they might turn to the Russians for support. The British, on the other hand, were turning to the Americans for help.

The Jewish 'Resistance Movement', as it was termed by the illegal Zionist radio station, renewed its activities and, in order to terminate their campaign, British troops occupied the offices of the Jewish Agency, arresting prominent Zionists, including Moshe Sharett (1894-1965), the Agency's head. Arms caches were seized and commanders of the paramilitary organisations were arrested. Matters escalated further when, on 22 July 1946, the Irgun ignited a bomb in the basement of the King David Hotel in Jerusalem, the British administrative headquarters for Palestine, killing 91 people, most of them Arab and Jewish civil servants. British public opinion was outraged but the attack did little to change the British approach to the Anglo-American agreement on Palestine, then in its final stages.

On 31 July, a Federal Plan was published for the division of Palestine into two districts, one Arab and one Jewish. Each grouping would manage its own affairs, including immigration which in the meantime continued illegally, many times the permitted quota arriving and being held in camps. When the British came up with a plan to transfer illegal immigrants to Cyprus, the ships used for this purpose were attacked by the Zionist paramilitaries. Negotiations on the Federal Plan continued with the Arabs proposing a state offering equal rights for all citizens but ending Jewish immigration.

In November, the arrested Zionists were released and a new wave of terrorism began with more British deaths. It ended, however, with the opening in December of the 22nd World Zionist Conference where the delegates demanded that Palestine be made a Jewish state and that 700,000 immigrants be allowed in so that there would be a Jewish majority in Palestine. Terrorist activity resumed the following January and, in February, a revised Federal Plan was rejected by both parties. At the end of April, the United Nations General Assembly considered the Palestine question in a special session, the terrorist campaign continuing in the background. A committee of representatives of countries with no interest in Palestine was set up and it recommended to the UN a Jewish state incorporating its present territory plus the Beersheba sub-district of Southern Palestine and Eastern Galilee. The Arabs would retain Western Galilee. It stipulated that, in the first two years, 150,000 Jewish immigrants should be allowed to enter Palestine. The problems included the fact that around 500,000 Arabs would be inside the Jewish state and, with the loss of Jaffa, the Arabs would have no port. They would also have to accept a higher rate of immigration than ever. Their independence would be conditional upon a guarantee by them of Jewish rights and the agreement to an economic union with the Jewish state, precluding any arrangements they might have wanted to make with other Arab countries.

In September, Britain declared that it would be unable to implement a policy that was not acceptable to both the Jews and the Arabs and would, therefore, be withdrawing its troops and closing down the British administration of Palestine. On 29 November, the United Nations approved the plans for partition of Palestine and fighting broke out almost immediately, the Arabs eager to demonstrate that they would not have the UN plan forced upon them without a struggle, and the Jews attempting to persuade the Arabs that such resistance was futile. When it became evident that the partition could not be achieved peacefully, the United Nations recommended that Palestine be placed under temporary UN trusteeship. On 14 May 1948, the day that the British Mandate on Palestine expired, the Jewish state of Israel was proclaimed by David Ben-Gurion, head of the World Zionist Organisation.

The 1948 Arab-Israeli War

On 15 May 1948, the day after the declaration of the new state, the UN Secretary-General, Trygve Lie (1896-1968), received a letter from the Secretary-General of the League of Arab States, Abdul Rahman Azzam (1893-1976), explaining that the nations of the League felt:

'... themselves compelled to intervene for the sole purpose of restoring peace and security and establishing law and order in Palestine... The governments of the Arab States hereby confirm at this stage the view that had been repeatedly declared by them on previous occasions... the only fair and just solution to the problem of Palestine is the creation of the United State of Palestine based upon the democratic principles...'

That same day, troops of Egypt, Lebanon, Syria, Jordan and Iraq moved against Israel, immediately seizing Arab areas and launching attacks on Israeli forces and several Israeli settlements. Lasting for ten months, the war took place mainly on the territory of the former British Mandate as well as briefly in the Sinai Peninsula and southern Lebanon. But the fledgling Israeli Defence Force was too strong for the Arabs and soon pushed them back beyond the borders they had established. By December 1948, Israel was in control of most of Mandate Palestine to the west of the River Jordan. On 24 February 1949, Egypt was the first of the invaders to sign an armistice with Israel, and the others soon followed. In 1949, Israel was admitted to the United Nations, declaring Jerusalem its capital although East Jerusalem still remained under Jordanian control, as agreed in the terms of the previous year's ceasefire agreement, Jordan having changed its name from Transjordan to the Hashemite Kingdom of Jordan.

At the end of the war, Israel had not only her own territory but also around 60 per cent of the land it was proposed would be given to the Arabs in the 1947 United Nations Partition Plan for Palestine. The gains included the areas of Jaffa, Lydda and Ramle, Galilee, parts of the Negev Desert area, West Jerusalem and lands on the West Bank. The rest of the British Mandate was annexed by Transjordan and Egypt took control of the Gaza Strip. The Jericho Conference of December 1948 demanded the unification of Palestine and Transjordan but, significantly, no separate state was provided for the Palestinian Arabs. Some 750,000 became refugees and, in 1949, the United Nations was providing relief rations to a million destitute Arabs. In the next three years around 700,000 Jews immigrated to the new State of Israel.

Post-War Egypt

The other big issue of the post-war Middle East was the presence in Egypt of British troops and the 'unity of the Nile Valley' – the independence of Sudan and its unity with Egypt. Although the Egyptian prime minister, Ismail Sidqi (1875-1950), acknowledged, as did King Farouk, that the Cold War made Egypt a strategically vital entity, and that the Anglo-Egyptian alliance was very much in their country's interest, many politicians and members of the media disagreed. The Wafd Party, which had been dismissed from government by the king in 1944, was encouraging unrest and the left of the party was working with the Soviets. Negotiations began in May 1946 and the British government offered to withdraw completely on condition that the two sides arrived at an agreement on mutual assistance. Eventually, Sidqi came to a compromise agreement with the British which hedged its bets on joint action to deal with threats in the Middle East. It also recognised 'unity between the Sudan and Egypt under the Egyptian crown'. The British insisted, however, that the Sudanese should be allowed to choose their own future and that the administration should remain in place there until they did so.

Sidqi neglected to mention this clause on his return to Egypt and the Egyptian people were wrongly convinced that all Sudanese were in favour of unity. The Sudanese Liberation Front encouraged violent demonstrations until the British persuaded them that the Sudanese people would be free to choose. The Egyptian prime minister resigned, to be replaced by Mahmoud Fahmi an-Nukrashi (1888-1948) who claimed that self-government 'in perpetual union with Egypt' was wanted by all Sudanese. When he proposed putting the matter to the United Nations, the British responded by announcing that they would revert to the 1936 Anglo-Egyptian Treaty until it expired in 1956. This meant retaining troops in the Canal Zone. Nukrashi's motion failed at the UN, not even gaining the votes of the USSR and Poland who were eager to see British troops withdraw from Egypt. Sudan's first legislature opened — without Egyptian blessing — in December 1948. The Egyptians remained intransigent on the matter, even after the re-election of the Wafd in January 1950 which might have been hoped to bring a better prospect of an agreement with the British.

Around this time, Egyptian ire began to be turned on King Abdullah of Transjordan who was believed to have British backing for his dream of a 'Greater Syria'. After the disaster of the 1948 conflict, the government of Syria was accused of being incompetent and corrupt, and the prime minister of Iraq, Nuri al-Said (1888-1958), began to pursue his idea of a union between Iraq and Syria with the aim of encouraging greater Arab unity in the future. But the Hashemite royal dynasty in Iraq and Jordan was unpopular with other Arab governments — Egypt, Saudi Arabia and Lebanon — and the Syrian army, which had perpetrated the first military overthrow in the Arab world following the Second World War (another two military coups followed that year), was opposed to the idea.

The Arab world was, therefore, in turmoil following the Arab-Israeli War of 1948. A million people had been turned into refugees and five years after the armistice there was little change, some fearing a reopening of hostilities. The British had unsuccessfully dreamed of creating a Middle East defence organisation that would act as a buffer to Soviet expansionist ambitions. By 1954, the government of the United States had instead started to create the possibility of a military alliance between Turkey and Pakistan. They hoped that a future Iraqi government might join this and lead other Arab states into membership.

Revolution in Egypt

Britain had been in control of Egypt in one way or another since the late nineteenth century. It had become a British Protectorate in 1914, had been granted independence of a sort in 1922 and, in 1936, the British had reached an agreement with the Egyptian government to withdraw all its troops to the Suez Canal zone, except in the event of war. During the Second World War, some Egyptian army officers had sided with the Nazis, the Germans promising that they would drive out the British if they won. This failed to materialise, of course, but there remained strong anti-British sentiment in Egypt, especially in the military.

King Farouk, the tenth monarch of the dynasty that had begun with Muhammad Ali, enjoyed a glamorous lifestyle and seemed to care more for his fleet of luxury cars than for the *fellahin* who lived in grinding poverty. This lifestyle, plus the fact that he appeared to be a puppet of the British and the corruption that surrounded him, led a group of officers of the Egyptian armed forces – known as the Free Officers Movement – to plot his overthrow. The Free Officers had formed in 1945 as a cell within the Muslim Brotherhood and remained a secret organisation of junior officers during the 1948 Arab-Israeli War. Amongst them was Egyptian army Major General Muhammad Naguib (1901-84), regarded as one of Egypt's few heroes of the 1948 war. Naguib would become Egypt's first president. Members included two other future Egyptian presidents – Gamal Abdel Nasser (1918-70) and Anwar Sadat. The Free Officers Movement had been fomenting agitation against the British for several years, including riots and attacks on British shipping and facilities. On 29 January 1952, in an atmosphere of crisis, Farouk dismissed the government. Three short-lived administrations followed until, on 22 July, the revolution was proclaimed on the radio in the name of General Naguib.

Less than 100 officers carried out the action and after it there were scenes of celebration on the streets of Cairo. Farouk was ordered to abdicate in favour of his son, Fuad II (r. 1952-53), and Nasser introduced a new constitution, forming a government not founded on Islamic principles but based on pan-Arab nationalism. Indeed, Nasser's regime would target Islamic radicals as well as communists and would prove to be repressive and authoritarian. Torture, assassination and incarceration without charge were common features. In 1953, the earlier constitution was abrogated and, on 18 June, Nasser declared Egypt a republic with Muhammad Naguib as its first president. Soon, all political parties had been banned apart from the government party, Liberation Rally. In autumn 1954, the Muslim Brotherhood was suppressed and then President Naguib was ousted from his position and arrested. He would spend the next eighteen years under house arrest. The Arab Socialist Nasser became president and would retain that position until his death in 1970.

The Suez Crisis

The Aswan Dam was an ambitious project that became a major objective of the new Egyptian government, which wanted to industrialise the country and have the ability to control the waters of the Nile, thus preventing flooding, managing irrigation and generating hydro-electricity. The United States and Great Britain offered to loan Egypt $270 million to finance the construction on condition that Nasser worked to solve the problems with Israel. Nasser had also asked the United States for weapons, much needed for defence against raids by Israeli troops. After United States President Dwight D. Eisenhower (1890-1969) told Nasser that, if the US gave him weapons, they could only be used for defensive purposes and would be supervised by American personnel, the ever-pragmatic Nasser turned to the Soviet Union, announcing an arms deal with the Russians. Eisenhower immediately withdrew the money promised for the dam. However, in an effort to restore good relations with Egypt, the Americans did make a contribution towards the construction of the dam. In June 1956, the Russians offered Egypt a loan of $1.2 billion for the dam and the United States withdrew completely. A week later, after Egyptian troops moved into the Suez Canal region and expelled the British, Nasser announced that the canal was to be nationalised.

Britain, of course, was in dire straits financially after the war and the government was not prepared simply to hand over the Suez Canal. Their presence in Egypt was strategically vital and allowed them to have a say in the Middle East. Demonstrating the importance of the canal to them, they had 80,000 troops in the region, and the vast military complex there was one of the biggest military bases in the world. For the French, also, the canal was of vital importance as a conduit for the oil reserves of the Middle East. Nonetheless, the seizure and nationalisation of the canal came as a complete surprise. Under great pressure, Prime Minister Anthony Eden (1897-1977) decided on military action, in collaboration with France and Israel. For Israel this represented a chance to strengthen its southern border and to weaken a hostile neighbouring state. The Israelis were also eager to strike at Egypt before Egypt used the large amount of weaponry it had obtained from the Soviet Union to attack them.

The Israelis launched an attack across the Sinai, forcing the Egyptian army to move forward to stop their advance. The British and French at this point issued an ultimatum demanding that both armies withdraw troops to at least ten kilometres from the canal. Nasser refused and the British and French began an aerial bombardment of Egyptian positions. It looked inevitable that the overwhelming strength of the Israelis, British and French would quickly prevail and, even when the two great Cold War rivals, the United States and the Soviet Union, joined forces to condemn the assault on Egypt, the invaders carried on regardless. Soon, British and French paratroops occupied the Suez Canal zone but domestic and international pressure began to mount. The Swedish Ambassador, Gunnar Hägglöf wrote to one Conservative MP:

> 'I don't think there is any part of the world where the sympathies for England are greater than in Scandinavia. But Scandinavian opinion has never been more shocked by a British government's action – not even by the British German Naval Agreement of 1935 – than by the Suez intervention.'

Having recently denounced the Soviet invasion of Hungary to quell the Hungarian Revolution, the United States felt it would be hypocritical to support the Franco-British action. Eisenhower also feared that to support it would throw the Arab states into the hands of the Russians. Therefore, he joined in an unlikely partnership with the Soviet Union to condemn the attack. The pressure eventually told and the European alliance was forced to abandon its occupation of the canal. Nasser was lauded by the Arab world for standing up to the Europeans.

Gamel Abdel Nasser died in 1970, still celebrated for his stance against what he and the Arab world viewed as Western imperialism. He had tried to pursue his vision of pan-Arab nationalism by negotiating in 1958 the merger of Syria and Egypt into the United Arab Republic but the Syrians walked away from the new venture in 1961. Part of his legacy, however, was the growth of Islamic militancy amongst those who suffered at the hands of his autocratic regime. These militants who began as enemies of Gamel Abdel Nasser would eventually turn the full power of their hatred against the West.

More Arab-Israeli Conflicts

Relations between Israel and its neighbours remained poor throughout the years following the war of 1948, but the situation deteriorated badly in the period leading up to their next confrontation in June 1967, the so-called Six Day War. There were numerous incidents over the years, involving both the Egyptians and the Syrians. Finally, in May 1967, President Nasser received reports from the USSR that Israel was massing troops on its border with Syria. The reports were untrue, but Nasser began to gather his own troops on the Israeli border in the Sinai. The Syrians were also preparing for war, and King Hussein of Jordan put his army under Egyptian control. Towards the end of May, Nasser closed the Gulf of Aqaba to Israeli ships. Describing this as an act of war, the Israelis formed a National Unity Government and at 7.45 am on 5 June, Israeli planes launched a massive surprise airstrike that destroyed the Egyptian, Syrian and Jordanian Air Forces before they could leave the ground. Around 450 aircraft were wrecked and 18 Egyptian airfields were put out of use, and the Israelis also quickly occupied the Sinai Peninsula. Egypt was beaten in three days, allowing the Israelis to attack Syria and Jordan. Within three days they had defeated them, too. They captured the Gaza Strip and the Sinai Peninsula from Egypt and the West Bank, East Jerusalem and the Golan Heights from Jordan. They began to build settlements on the land they had captured, which has been a point of contention between the Arabs and Israelis ever since.

SHIFTING SANDS

Six years later, in the Yom Kippur War (known to Arabs as the Ramadan War), the Arabs were better prepared and had Soviet support. Nasser died of a heart attack in 1970 and was succeeded by Anwar Sadat who, although appearing to be a moderate, desperately wanted to avenge the 1967 defeat and to retake Sinai. On 6 October 1973 – the eve of Yom Kippur, the holiest day for Jewish people – Egypt launched surprise attacks on Israeli troops in the Golan Heights and the Sinai Desert. They enjoyed great success in the Sinai, overrunning Israeli positions, and meanwhile the Syrians seized part of the Golan Heights. Israeli Prime Minister, Golda Meir (1898-1978), appealed to the United States for help and President Richard Nixon (1913-94) obliged by sending military supplies. The Soviets did the same for Egypt. Cold War tensions were heightened when the Russians announced they were about to send airborne divisions to help the Egyptians and, at one point during the conflict, America was on nuclear alert, the closest the world had come to nuclear warfare since the Cuban Missile Crisis of 1962. A ceasefire was declared on 25 October, by which time Israel had managed to reoccupy the Golan Heights and seize most of the Sinai. There were serious implications to this war. The Arabs, humiliated by their defeat in the Six Day War, were buoyed by their early successes in the Yom Kippur War. The Israelis, although they had eventually performed well on the battlefield, realised from the setbacks they had suffered that they would perhaps not always prevail militarily over their Arab neighbours and that it might be wise to try diplomacy. Thus, the two sides engaged in a peace process that resulted in the Camp David Accords of 1978. Sinai was returned to Egypt and Egypt became the first Arab country to recognise Israel. But the Yom Kippur War was something of a watershed for Israel. On its founding it had been feted by the world as a country peopled by refugees from the horror of the Holocaust. In the 1970s, however, the world began to turn against her. In November 1973, for example, the European Community demanded that Israel withdraw from the Arab territories it was occupying.

The oil embargo of the 1970s demonstrated to the Arabs the power that they had and they began to use oil as a weapon, resulting in the United Nations passing measures that named the Palestine Liberation Organisation (PLO) the 'government in exile' of the Palestinian people. The PLO, a terrorist organisation responsible for a number of high-profile hijackings, assassinations and bombings in Israel, explicitly wanted the destruction of Israel. It was understandable, therefore, that Israeli Prime Minister Yitzhak Rabin (1922-95) said that Israel would not be able to negotiate with representatives of the organisation.

In 1975, Israel was dealt a further blow when the United Nations passed a resolution – sponsored by the USSR and the Arab nations – that declared Zionism to be a form of racism. It was rescinded in 1991, but Israel was becoming increasingly dependent on the United States as virtually its only friend.

Iraq Becomes a Republic

At the end of the Second World War, Iraq's economy was in a parlous state and shortages were so bad that there was famine in one part of the country. In 1947, Prime Minister Salih Jabr (1896-1957), Iraq's first Shiite prime minister, revisited the 1930 Anglo-Iraqi Treaty with Britain with a view to ending the country's relationship with the British and forcing them to leave. The Treaty of Portsmouth, signed in January 1948, guaranteed that the British would, indeed, withdraw from Iraq, but they would advise on military matters for the next 25 years. Outraged

Iraqis rioted in the streets of Baghdad. Prince Abd al-Ilah (1913-58), the regent for the 12-year-old King Faisal II (r. 1935-58), replaced Jabr with another Shiite, Mohammed al-Sadr (1882-1956).

When the Arabs went to war with Israel in 1948, Iraq contributed the largest number of troops, more than 20,000 and, after the tide turned against the Arab cause, the Iraqi government began to take it out on the country's Jews, around 2 per cent of the population, who were harassed and arrested. There were even some executions, although wartime events in Europe were still fresh in the world's mind and Iraq was stopped from perpetrating even harsher treatment by the international outcry. Needless to say, many of Iraq's Jews immigrated to Israel.

By the mid-1950s, with Nuri al-Said once again prime minister, Iraq began to benefit from the more favourable division of oil profits that it had negotiated. Meanwhile, opposition to the government was ruthlessly dealt with and all political parties were banned. This led to a coalition of opposition groups forming the United National Front (UNF). The members had little in common apart from the desire to remove Nuri al-Said from government.

Amongst the disparate organisations that made up the coalition was the Ba'ath (meaning 'Revival' in Arabic) Party, founded in Syria in the 1940s. It was a generally secular party with slightly socialist tendencies, concerned with righting the injustices and inequalities in Iraqi society. The UNF began to gain the support of officers in the Iraqi armed forces and momentum gathered behind an organisation known as the Free Officers and Civilians Movement. They planned a coup, at the head of which were Brigadier-General Abd al-Karim Qasim (1914-63) and Colonel Abd al-Salam Arif (1921-66).

When Egypt and Syria joined together to form the United Arab Republic in 1958, Iraq hastily cobbled together a union with Jordan – the Arab Union – to counter the threat posed on its border. Nuri al-Said was appointed prime minister of the new union. Shortly afterwards, however, the UNF launched its coup, declaring Iraq a 'sovereign republic'. The royal palace was attacked and the king and his family were shot dead. Nuri al-Said was killed as he tried to flee dressed as a woman. His body was dismembered and carried in triumph through the streets of Baghdad.

The Rise of Saddam Hussein

Qasim proclaimed the coup to be a 'mass revolution' even though it was far from that. Little had changed, apart from the absence of the monarchy. The army still governed and the Sunnis, as ever, were in charge. As prime minister, minister of defence and commander-in-chief, he purged the officer ranks of the armed forces of pan-Arab sympathisers. Meanwhile, he and his cohorts ensured that a percentage of the country's oil profits found their way to Swiss bank accounts. In October 1959, the Ba'ath Party tried to assassinate him, an act that only served to make him even more ruthless. Qasim also antagonised the countries around him and Iraq soon had few friends in the Middle East. He was forced to turn to the Soviet Union for financial aid and military equipment.

In the early 1960s, opposition groups began to devise plans for a coup. The Kurdish Democratic Party made peace with the Ba'ath Party and both united against Qasim. In February 1963, the coup was launched and Qasim was captured and executed. The Ba'athists established a government – the National Council of Revolutionary Command – the president of which was Qasim's erstwhile deputy Abd al-Salam Arif who had been imprisoned by his old associate. The council was made up of Ba'athists and Arab nationalists but it was a brutal period with some 3,000 people in opposition groups being murdered. Arif was killed in a plane crash in 1966 and was replaced by his brother Abdul al-Rahman Arif (1916-2007). Two years later, however, Hasan al-Bakr (1914-82) led a coup that sent Abdul Arif into exile. Al-Bakr appointed a relative, Saddam Hussein (1937-2006), as head of national security, a role that he relished, displaying a penchant for torture and public executions.

For some time, Iran and Iraq had been baiting each other, the shah jealously eyeing the Shatt al-Arab waterway to a large section of which he laid a claim. The problems the Iraqi regime had with the Kurds and the Shiites – Iran being predominantly Shiite – did not help. Eventually, after the Kurds had seriously damaged Iraqi oil operations at Kirkuk, negotiations were held between Mustafa Barzani (1903-79), the Kurd leader, and Saddam Hussein as a result of which the Iraqis agreed to recognise the Kurds as a distinct nationality within Iraq. They were given a degree of autonomy and, in return, agreed to stop accepting Iranian military aid. But Saddam had little intention of sticking to his side of the bargain and efforts were made to weaken the Kurds. In 1971, there were several attempts on Barzani's life. The government denied involvement, but Barzani gradually began once again to accept support from the shah. By 1974, Iranian and Iraqi troops were involved in skirmishes along their common border and the Kurds were attacking Iraqi facilities on behalf of Teheran. Trying to avoid a major conflict, the two sides negotiated an agreement, and Iran was granted additional territory in the Shatt al-Arab in return for an Iranian pledge to stop funding the Kurdish fighters in northern Iraq. The Kurds were abandoned and their uprising was over.

It was a prosperous time for Iraq. Al-Bakr nationalised the Iraqi Petroleum Company in 1972 and oil prices soared throughout the 1970s. The government introduced free health care, free education and other benefits. In 1977, Saddam, now the leading power in the party, made two important moves that would lead to his takeover of the country. He took total control of Iraq's petroleum industry and he banned all non-Ba'athist political activity in the armed forces. He also made some important moves in foreign policy, distancing Iraq from Moscow, although continuing to rely on the Russians as the country's top arms suppliers. He also severed relations with Egypt after President Anwar Sadat visited Jerusalem in 1977; Saddam hated Israel. In October 1978, he began to befriend Syria, also ruled by the Ba'ath Party and as anti-Israel as Saddam.

Saddam was vehemently opposed to outright union with Syria. Therefore, when al-Bakr began to devise treaties with Syria that would make the Syrian president deputy-leader of the union, he was concerned. Such a move would push him to one side, frustrating his leadership ambitions. He acted decisively. On 16 July 1979, he persuaded the ailing al-Bakr to resign and became president. He arrested and tortured those in his party who opposed him and, of the 68 arrested, 22 were executed. Hundreds more would die in the coming weeks. Saddam Hussein began to stake his claim for leadership of the country.

Iran After the Second World War

Throughout the Second World War, Iran was occupied by the British, the Russians and a small contingent of Americans, leaving the new shah with little say in his country's affairs. At the war's conclusion, however, the Americans were particularly eager to see the Russians leave the country. They had introduced Marxism to the region and had done everything to increase the influence of Moscow whilst also encouraging bad feeling towards the central government amongst the Azeris and the Kurds. President Truman ordered the withdrawal of all American troops and demanded the Soviets do the same by 1 March 1946. The Russians ignored this deadline, even though Britain was also withdrawing her forces. As a Soviet-controlled Iranian political party, the Tudeh, began organising strikes and demonstrations in Teheran, the Soviet leader, Josef Stalin (1878-1953), was giving speeches that talked about the need for Iran to be liberated. Truman put US forces based in Austria on high alert, forcing Stalin to back down and order the withdrawal of Soviet troops.

The British government was still the biggest shareholder in the Anglo-Iranian Oil Company and it seemed in Iran that Britain was still acting like a colonial power. There were strikes by the company's workers and a fleet of British warships was dispatched to Iran. But the British were not alone in being disliked by Iranians. The shah, too, was unpopular, surviving an assassination attempt in 1949 believed to have been instigated by the disgruntled clergy. It persuaded the shah to take more action against the religious conservatives and communists. Those against him united — liberals and conservatives finding common ground in their hatred for him and the Anglo-Iranian Oil Company — and formed the National Front. Its leader was Mohammed Mosaddegh (1882-1967), a member of parliament and a passionate Iranian nationalist.

Under pressure from the National Front, the Iranian government demanded that the terms of the agreement with the AIOC be renegotiated. They were demanding 50 per cent of the profits but the British, in financial difficulties following the war, and still with a colonial view of the world, offered only a very small increase in Iran's share. The proposal was rejected by the Iranian Parliament which passed a nationalisation measure that the shah unwillingly approved. Outraged, the British government readied an invasion force of 70,000 troops. Concerned that such an act would drive Iran into the Soviet camp, President Truman denounced the plan and told British Prime Minister Clement Attlee (1883-1967) that the United States would not give him its support for an invasion. US government officials also began expressing support for Mosaddegh, although he responded by telling the Americans to stop meddling in Iranian affairs.

In 1951, Iran nationalised its oilfields but a subsequent embargo placed on Iranian oil brought a crisis, with production reduced and thousands of workers losing their jobs. Elections the following year went badly for the National Front as the religious faction withdrew from the coalition opposed to the shah. In Britain, Prime Minister Winston Churchill used Britain's involvement in the Korean crisis as leverage for American support in finding a solution to the crisis in Iran. The situation deteriorated as rioting broke out following Mosaddegh's resignation from parliament, and the shah responded by dismissing his prime minister and installing Mosaddegh in the role. Mosaddegh immediately declared martial law and introduced 'emergency powers'. The constitution was suspended and he began to get rid of the opposition.

Truman persuaded Britain to agree to a 50-50 share of Iranian oil profits, but Mosaddegh declined the offer, demanding 50 million dollars in compensation as a condition of accepting the deal. He threatened the new US President Dwight D. Eisenhower that Iran would turn to the Soviets for help if the dispute with Britain remained unresolved. It was a fatal miscalculation, leading the Americans to begin to plan Mosaddegh's downfall in an initiative named Operation Ajax. Working with Britain's MI6, the CIA identified a prospective replacement for Mosaddegh — the royalist Iranian General Fazlollah Zahedi (1897-1963). With a campaign of propaganda and infiltration as well as economic sanctions in August 1953, they succeeded in toppling Mosaddegh and replacing him with Zahedi. There were riots, forcing the shah to flee the country, but eventually the royalists came out on top and Mosaddegh was arrested, remaining under house arrest until his death in 1967, a hero to ordinary Iranians. The secret overthrow of Mosaddegh became an important factor in anti-United States protests during the 1979 Iranian Revolution.

Iran's White Revolution

Where once it had been communists the shah had feared, increasingly it was Islamic fundamentalists who posed the greatest threat. In 1957, he established the National Intelligence and Security Organisation (SAVAK), a secret police force trained by the CIA and Israel's Mossad. It was created to keep an eye on the shah's enemies and its officers had wide-ranging powers of arrest and detention. Torture was frequently used, and assassinations and executions were common.

In 1963, in an effort to modernise Iran, the shah launched the White Revolution, a series of reforms that antagonised the clergy even further. Its main features were women's suffrage and educational and land reform, the latter aimed directly at the clergy who were major landowners. Their land was confiscated and redistributed or it was converted to public use. Women were given the right to vote and run for public office and religion was purged from the education system. These were initiatives aimed partly at establishing better relations with the nation's peasantry and legitimising the shah's regime. But there were many improvements. Port facilities were upgraded and the country's infrastructure was expanded. Factories were built, enrolment in education increased and literacy rose from 26 to 42 per cent. However, the revolution also increased the educated classes who opposed the shah, and land reform created large numbers of individual farmers and landless labourers who felt little affinity with him. The oil wealth became concentrated in the hands of a few and failed to trickle down to the masses. This type of corruption angered many who still felt loyal to the mullahs especially in view of the unemployment and shortage of houses and food. The resulting unrest helped to bring about the rise of an Ayatollah who would be an outspoken critic of the shah and would play an important role in Iran's future – Ruhollah Khomeini (1902-89).

This was all in spite of a sharp rise in oil revenue as the world's demand for oil grew. The shah squandered the money trying to turn Iran into the most advanced military power in the Middle East. Finally, America stopped providing aid because the country was now considered quite capable of standing on its own two feet. From the now discredited National Front emerged opposition groups, most of them Islamic. Although incapable of overthrowing the increasingly unpopular government, they engaged in acts of terrorism including bombings and the assassination of politicians.

The Fall of the Shah

With the Iranian economy in turmoil, the shah strove to make the most of his oil revenues. In 1973, the Organisation of Petroleum Exporting Countries (OPEC) announced an oil embargo, a response to American involvement in the Yom Kippur War. The embargo was enacted against the United States, Canada, Japan, the Netherlands and the United Kingdom. Prices were also increased. The shah was reported as saying in the *New York Times*:

'Of course [the world price of oil] is going to rise... Certainly! and how... you [the countries of the West] increased the price of wheat you sell us by 300 per cent and the same for sugar and cement... You buy our crude oil and sell it back to us refined as petrochemicals at a hundred times the price you've paid to us... it's only fair that, from now on you should pay more for oil. Let's say ten times more.'

US President Nixon was furious but was unable to persuade him to back down on oil prices. The increases, of course, brought money flooding into Iran, but the shah continued to squander it on expensive military hardware. Corruption in the government remained a huge problem and this was against a background of shortages due to failed agricultural policies and a lack of housing. SAVAK terrorised Iranians, and opposition to the regime was dealt with ruthlessly. Many ordinary Iranians turned to religion and, since mosques were the only places where SAVAK agents were not active, they became the only places where free speech was possible. Islam proved an alternative to the shah and people began to adopt the Islamic style of dress, men growing beards and women wearing the veil once more. Around 1977, the shah learned that he had terminal cancer. He wanted to ensure that his son would succeed him but Iran was in turmoil. He edged towards reform and placed limits on the powers of SAVAK. But it was too little, too late.

Events soon began to spiral out of control. In August 1977, there were violent clashes after the Mayor of Teheran demolished impoverished neighbourhoods without notice in order to build a motorway. The following October, Ayatollah Khomeini's son was killed in Iraq, a murder that some believed to have been perpetrated by agents acting for the shah. In November, the shah visited the White House where violent demonstrations involving thousands of Iranian students studying in the United States broke out. In January 1978, Jimmy Carter (1924-2024) visited Teheran, giving rise to more speculation that the shah was a US puppet.

In early 1978, the Iranian government made efforts to turn the country against the exiled Ayatollah Khomeini who took every opportunity to denounce the shah. A newspaper editorial led to the customary riots but it also raised the profile of the powerful mullah. Cassette tapes of him railing against the shah, the Americans and Israel sold in tens of thousands. Meanwhile, the demonstrations were becoming increasingly serious. On 8 September 1978 – 'Black Friday' – police opened fire on demonstrators in Teheran's Jaleh Square, killing many. It was the point of no return; there could now be no compromise between the shah and his opponents, and he declared martial law.

By the autumn of 1978, the regime was in serious trouble. Islamists had taken control of the northern city of Babol and oil workers went on strike. Soldiers began to desert in huge numbers. Finally, in 1979, the shah and his wife boarded a plane and flew into exile, never to return.

The Return of the Ayatollah

Ayatollah Khomeini returned to Iran on 2 February 1979, 15 years after being sent into exile by the government. He returned with the objective of establishing the first Islamic state since the lifetime of the Prophet. He positioned himself as the authority on how to do this, establishing a cult of personality, something that amounted to blasphemy to many Muslims. A clash with the hated enemy, the United States, was inevitable and it began when Khomeini announced that he wanted to put the shah on trial. This was, of course, impossible, given that the shah had taken refuge in America, confirming to many Iranians that he had, indeed, been conspiring with the Americans. A mob gathered in front of the US embassy in Teheran, demanding the return of the monarch, and, on 4 November, it broke through the perimeter, taking 52 American hostages. Lasting 444 days, this hostage crisis was a traumatic event for the United States, gravely damaging the presidency of Jimmy Carter. At last Iran was able to avenge herself on what it perceived as the injustices done to her by the West – secularisation, the exploitation of her oil reserves and the CIA-backed coup of 1953 that brought down Mosaddegh's government.

President Carter decided that a military attack would prove too dangerous for the hostages. Therefore, he tried to isolate Iran diplomatically, attempting to gain acceptance for sanctions, but America's allies were reluctant to antagonise a major oil producer. The situation became even more difficult following the Soviet Union's invasion of Afghanistan in December 1979. The age-old fear of driving Iran into Soviet hands was raised once more and there was even fear that a military attack might provoke the Soviets to invade Iran as well. A rescue attempt by the US Army Delta Force failed disastrously.

If things were going badly for Carter – he was about to lose the presidential election to Ronald Reagan (1911-2004) – they were also turning nasty for the Ayatollah. Even at that point, however, Khomeini was determined to see Jimmy Carter suffer, holding on to the hostages (now a desperate liability) just long enough for the American people to express their disappointment in Carter at the ballot box. The Iranians rubbed salt in Carter's wounds by releasing the hostages on 21 January 1981, the day of Ronald Reagan's inauguration, but not before he had been sworn in as president.

In the early 1980s, Khomeini believed that his Islamic Revolution could be exported to other Middle Eastern countries. Lebanon was one such place, with its large number of Shiites and weak government. It had been victim to a number of incursions by the Israelis and suffered from sectarian pressures. Madrasas

– Islamic schools – were funded by Iran in Lebanon and their graduates joined groups such as Hezbollah, the Shiite militant and political organisation. These groups began launching terrorist attacks and taking Western hostages. There was little new US President Ronald Reagan could do.

Ayatollah Khomeini died in 1989 and, in an outpouring of grief, several million Iranians attended his funeral. He was replaced as Supreme Leader by another cleric, Ali Khamenei (b. 1939) and Hashemi Rafsanjani (1934-2017) took office as president. Rafsanjani was followed as president by the moderate reformist Mohammad Khatami (b. 1943) but the 2005 presidential elections returned a conservative, Mahmoud Ahmadinejad (b. 1956). In 2013, Hassan Rouhani (b. 1948) was elected president and he has improved Iran's relations with other countries including the United States. In 2015, an agreement was reached on an understanding to limit Iran's nuclear programmes, long a contentious issue in global politics.

The Iran-Iraq War

Although Iraq was one of the first countries to recognise Ayatollah Khomeini's Islamic republic, the Ayatollah had little time for Saddam Hussein's secular state. By 1980, Saddam was still smarting from the concessions on Shatt al-Arab that had been made to Iran five years previously and wanted to regain the territory Iraq had lost. He also aspired to be the leader of the Arab Sunni world and a strike against the Shiite Iran would help his cause. He decided to try to capture the oil-rich province of Khuzestan, just across the Iranian border. Oil was at record prices and seizure of this territory would bring a huge boost to the already flourishing Iraqi economy. It was the right moment. The shah had spent billions on military hardware from the United States but the Americans were now refusing to sell Iran spare parts or ammunition and it was all becoming useless. The Iranian army had deteriorated badly since the revolution, a fact not helped by Khomeini's purges of hundreds of officers on ideological grounds.

In September 1980, Saddam ripped up the 1975 Algiers Accord that had settled border disputes between Iran and Iraq and declared that the entire Shatt al-Arab belonged to Iraq. Planning a quick war, he launched it with the tactic that had enabled Israel to defeat Egypt in the 1967 Six Day War – destroying the enemy's aircraft on the ground. Unfortunately Iraqi airmen were not up to the job, failing to find their targets or hitting the wrong ones. On the ground the Iraqi army fared little better, its officers often political appointees who knew little about warfare. Moreover, Saddam had failed to account for the revolutionary and religious fervour of the young men of Iran. Waves of them, seeking martyrdom, were thrown into battle. As the war began to go badly for Iraq, Saddam began to panic and suggested to the Iranians that the two Muslim nations should unite and attack their common enemy, Israel. Khomeini decided instead to continue the conflict in order to overthrow Saddam. He would then move on to liberate Jerusalem. Many of his officers opposed the plan but Khomeini was all-powerful and Iran made preparations for the invasion of Iraq, starting in Basra. Saddam restored many of the professional officers he had dismissed and purchased expensive, sophisticated weapons and, after two weeks of brutal combat, Khomeini withdrew his troops from southern Iraq.

The Saudi Arabian rulers, fearing that if Iran defeated Iraq they would be next, proposed a peace settlement that included $70 billion in reparations to Iran. Saddam was keen on this if it meant no more Iranian invasions but the Ayatollah rejected the offer. The war continued and, as the oil prices declined, Saddam fought using loans from Saudi Arabia and Kuwait. Amongst his purchases were chemical weapons that his troops deployed as early in the conflict as 1984.

Concerned at a potential disruption to oil supplies, and still smarting after the hostage crisis, the United States began to provide military aid to Iraq. Outraged Americans learned in 1986 from the Iran-Contra scandal that their government had also been supplying weapons to Iran. Senior officials in the Reagan administration had secretly facilitated the sale of arms to Iran in order to secure the release of hostages and to fund the rebel group, the Contras, which was trying to overthrow the Sandinista government in Nicaragua. Somewhat bizarrely, Israel was involved too, helping to supply weapons to Teheran because it felt that Saddam's Iraq represented a bigger threat to peace. The supply of weapons to Iran turned the war in their favour and they came close to taking Basra.

The Iranians tried to dissuade Gulf States' leaders from funding Iraq's war effort by bombing their tankers in the Persian Gulf and installed missile launch sites on the Straits of Hormuz that could decimate traffic in the Gulf. The Kuwaitis proposed sailing their tankers under the American flag, guaranteeing them the protection of the US Navy but the Reagan administration rejected the idea, forcing the Kuwaitis to turn to the Soviet Union. Within a few weeks their tankers were sailing under the hammer and sickle of the USSR. Soon after, however, an Iraqi Mirage fighter mistakenly fired missiles at the USS *Stark*, killing 37 American sailors. Washington was, unsurprisingly, furious, but turned its ire on Iran for making the Persian Gulf part of the conflict. President Reagan permitted Iraqi fighters to fly under the US flag, bringing the US Navy into the war, providing protection for tankers. When

Kuwaiti tankers started to become victims of mines deposited in the Gulf by Iran, America responded decisively. For the last year of the conflict the United States was virtually at war with Iran.

Domestically, however, life was becoming difficult and the Iranian people's enthusiasm for their revolution was beginning to wane. The leadership realised it had to find a way to end the war. For Saddam, too, continuance of the fighting was becoming a thorny matter within the Iraqi military. As Khomeini faced dissent amongst his generals, the Iranian military was running out of resources and he was persuaded to agree to a United Nations-brokered ceasefire. The Algiers Accord of 1975 was reinstated and the $200 billion dollars and half a million lives that the war had cost the two countries had changed nothing.

The Build-up to the Gulf War

Even while Iraq was fighting Iran, Saddam was also dealing with the Kurds in northern Iraq. An uprising in 1986 was met with a terror campaign by his troops. Farms and villages were torched and mass executions perpetrated. Chemical weapons were also used, and the senior government figure involved, Ali Hassan al-Majid (1941-2010), became known as 'Chemical Ali'.

Meanwhile, Iraq was in the midst of an economic crisis, owing billions of dollars to the Gulf States for loans during the war. Saddam also had to fund the reconstruction of parts of Iraq following the war, but was still spending vast sums on arms. Iraq was dependent on imports, having no manufacturing base of its own. Of course, the country exported large quantities of oil, but the price of oil was low and Saddam was unable to persuade his fellow OPEC members to raise prices. Owing a great deal of money, in particular to Kuwait, Saddam decided that the only way to get his country back in the black was to invade the oil-rich Gulf state. Then, he believed, he could start to threaten Saudi Arabia, to whom Iraq was also indebted and have that debt expunged. He massed forces along the Kuwaiti border and reiterated his demands to the Kuwaiti royal family. They met him halfway, but it was not enough for Saddam. Convinced that the Americans would shy away from involvement in a war in the Middle East, he sent 100,000 battle-hardened troops into Kuwait on 2 August 1990. Twenty-four hours later they had taken the country, claiming that they had done it to 'save the Kuwaiti monarchy from traitors'. Kuwait was proclaimed the 19th province of Iraq.

The world was outraged. The United Nations ordered Saddam to withdraw his troops and placed a trade embargo on Iraq while Iraqi and Kuwaiti assets in banks worldwide were frozen. Iraq's oil pipelines through Turkey and Saudi Arabia were switched off. In Baghdad, Saddam outraged the world by detaining a group of Western expatriates as 'human shields'. Somewhat ridiculously, he told the hostages, 'Your presence here, and in other places, is meant to prevent the scourge of war.'

The First Gulf War

On 29 November 1990, the United Nations passed Resolution 678, authorising the use of force to expel Iraqi troops from Kuwait, the deadline for an Iraqi withdrawal being 15 January 1991. As the deadline approached, a remarkable coalition was assembled to expel the Iraqi forces from Kuwait. Soldiers from the Muslim world – Syria, Pakistan, Oman, Egypt, Qatar and Bahrain – lined up with troops from the United States, Great Britain, and France.

It must be remembered that Iraq's troops had been battle-hardened by the long years of war with Iran, and Iraq had one of the largest armies in the world. A land war was, therefore, not an option for the coalition. However, Iraq's air defences were poor. For that reason, Operation Desert Storm began with an attack from the air on 16 January, the day after the deadline had expired. The aerial bombardment continued for six weeks. Israel remained neutral in the conflict as no Arab state was likely to want to fight alongside Israeli troops but Saddam tried to involve her by firing Scud missiles at her cities. The Israeli government showed remarkable restraint in refusing to respond to the attacks, much to the relief of US President George H.W. Bush (1924-2018). On 24 February, ground troops moved in and rolled over the weakened Iraqi forces. In Kuwait, the retreating Iraqi troops set fire to oil wells, causing damage that would take months to put right and creating an environmental disaster. The war was won in days but President Bush decided that the job should be limited to clearing Iraq's forces from Kuwait. Controversially, Saddam remained in place. The ceasefire was signed on 28 February 1991.

The war had cost Iraq 45,000 lives and more than $200 billion. The coalition, on the other hand, suffered only 450 casualties and expenditure amounted to only $82 billion. In Iraq, after the war, there were uprisings by Shiite groups but they were poorly coordinated and were quelled by Saddam's elite Republican Guards. The United Nations introduced sanctions that lasted for the next decade. But Saddam held on to power in Iraq.

Civil War and Revolution in Lebanon

The Lebanese Civil War lasted from 1975 to 1990, at a cost of an estimated 120,000 casualties. Lebanon had been multi-sectarian, the coast populated by mostly Sunnis and Christians, while Shiites were to be found mainly in the south and the Beqaa Valley to the west. In the mountains lived the Druze and Christians. The parliamentary structure favoured the Christians, and the large Muslim population disliked the government's pro-Western stance.

The Maronite Christians and the Palestinians began fighting in 1975, the Palestinians being supported by pan-Arab sympathisers and Muslims. Other countries became involved; the Syrians went into Lebanon in what was described as a peacekeeping role on behalf of the Arab League but actually threw their support behind the Muslims and targeted the Christians. Israel supported a Maronite Christian right-wing group known as the Phalangists and made incursions into Lebanon to deal with PLO bases there. When Syrian helicopters were found to be attacking Phalangists, Israeli fighters were sent to destroy them. Syria stationed surface-to-air missiles in the Beqaa Valley and Israel delivered an ultimatum to the Syrian government to remove them. The Syrians refused, moving more troops and missiles into the area. Mediation by US Special Envoy Philip Habib (1920-92) narrowly averted a major confrontation.

Attacks on Israel by the PLO from inside Lebanon finally drove the Israelis to take action. On 6 June 1982, they launched airstrikes against PLO bases as well as Syrian forces. The Israeli Defence Force took possession of much of the south of Lebanon, capturing around 10,000 prisoners who were held in detention camps. Once again Philip Habib brokered a ceasefire. An agreement was reached whereby the PLO would be withdrawn from southern Lebanon, but their places were quickly filled with Shiite fighters.

The Israelis returned to Lebanon in September 1982 to maintain order after the assassination of the Phalangist leader, Bachir Gemayel (1947-82), who had been elected president of Lebanon but had been killed before he could take office. Meanwhile, there was tragedy in the Israeli detention camps in

September 1982 when Christian Phalangist militia entered two of them – Sabra and Shatila – and massacred the inhabitants, including women and children. It was later found that the Israeli officers in charge of the camps could have done more to prevent the atrocity. The Israeli Minister of Defence, Ariel Sharon (1928-2014), was forced to resign his position.

Following the assassination of the former Lebanese Prime Minister Rafik Hariri (1944-2005) in February 2005, there were demonstrations across the country, especially in Beirut. The demonstrators called for the withdrawal of the 14,000 Syrian troops still based in Lebanon and the removal of the pro-Syrian government. The movement, named the Cedar Revolution, involved a number of civilian and political groups. In response to the protests and international pressure, Syrian troops were withdrawn after 30 years in Lebanon and the government resigned on 28 February.

Peace Efforts

Attempts to find peace in the Middle East went on, of course, for decades. In 1978, US President Jimmy Carter decided on a more proactive approach to Middle East politics. In office in Israel was Menachem Begin (1913-92), founder of the conservative Likud Party. He was eager to see peace with Egypt, but unwilling to give an inch on the ongoing problem of Israeli settlements in the Occupied Territories. A meeting was planned at the president's retreat at Camp David in Maryland. Meanwhile, the Egyptian President Anwar Sadat made a momentous trip to Israel in 1977 and gave a speech in the Knesset. Although he merely reiterated the Egyptian position, it was a highly significant occasion. Islamic fundamentalists were, of course, outraged and four years later they would vent their anger by assassinating Sadat.

In September 1978, Sadat and Begin met with Carter at Camp David, and discussions continued for 13 days before they emerged with two new agreements – the Framework for the Conclusion of a Peace Treaty between Egypt and Israel and the Framework for Peace in the Middle East. These agreements stipulated that Israel would withdraw from the Sinai and that Egypt would acknowledge Israel's right to exist. Diplomatic relations were also to be re-established and each country agreed that talks would be held in the future to discuss Palestine. It was an agreement that made Egypt extremely unpopular with its Arab neighbours and the country's membership of the Arab League was suspended until 1989. For the Egyptians it was beneficial, as they not only got the Sinai Desert back but also received American aid.

When Bill Clinton (b. 1946) became president of the United States in 1993, he made a pledge that he would bring the conflict between the Israelis and the Palestinians to an end by the conclusion of his first year in office. The situation had been deteriorating, and rioting by the Palestinians towards the end of 1987 – the First Intifada – had resulted in the deaths of more than 1,400 Palestinians. A year later, Yasser Arafat (1929-2004), the Palestinian leader, announced that the PLO was renouncing terrorism and was recognising the right of the state of Israel to exist. The Reagan administration in Washington moved towards talks with the PLO. Meanwhile, the issue of Jewish settlements in the Occupied Territories was becoming serious. Mikhail Gorbachev (1931-2022) had come to power in Moscow and, as part of his liberalisation of the Soviet regime, he allowed Russian Jews to emigrate to Israel. There was pressure, therefore, for housing. Against this background, a peace conference was organised in Madrid involving representatives from Israel, Syria and Lebanon. There were Palestinians present but they were not from the PLO. Needless to say, no major breakthroughs occurred.

Clinton had expressed support for Israel during his presidential campaign, acknowledging that it had a right to exist and to defend itself. He sent his experienced Secretary of State Warren Christopher (1925-2011) to the Middle East at a time when the situation was particularly fraught. This led to talks between Israel and the PLO in Oslo in Norway as a result of which they agreed to recognise each other's right to exist. In December 1993, Israel and the PLO signed the Declaration of Principles on Interim Self-Government Arrangements at the White House. By this, Israel would withdraw from the Gaza Strip within five years and Palestinians living in the West Bank would be granted some autonomy. The PLO promised to renounce terrorism as the means to achieve its goals and agreed to recognise Israel.

The Palestinians, therefore, needed a governmental apparatus. The Palestinian Authority was given this role on a temporary basis but Israel and the Authority would enter into negotiations to determine the nature of Palestinian statehood. Issues remained but it did represent progress and, in September 1995, the two sides signed the Israeli-Palestinian Interim Agreement. This became known as Oslo II, the entire series of agreements being called the Oslo Accords. Meanwhile, Israel and Jordan signed a peace agreement at the White House on 26 October 1994 which established diplomatic relations between the two countries.

The optimism surrounding these advances in Middle East relations was dented by the assassination of the Israeli premier, Yitzhak Rabin, who had played such a huge role in the Oslo Accords. His successor, Shimon Peres (1923-2016), lacked the political substance and the ability to broker deals with the Palestinians that Rabin had. The Palestinians, too, had difficulties. When the PLO became the Palestinian Authority and rejected terrorism, many Palestinians became disgruntled and moved their loyalties to another resistance movement active on the West Bank – Hamas.

Efforts continued elsewhere and, in March 2000, Israeli Prime Minister Ehud Barak (b. 1942) controversially withdrew Israeli troops from Lebanon, partly in order to placate Syria, whose substantial arsenal was now a major military threat to Israel. The unanticipated result was that the Lebanese terrorist group Hezbollah strengthened in southern Lebanon and its activities would force Israel to invade the region once again in 2006.

But the arguments over Israeli settlements and the right of return for Palestinian refugees were ongoing. At a meeting – known as Camp David II – between President Clinton, Prime Minister Barak and Yasser Arafat in July 2000, the Palestinian leader rejected an offer of 95 per cent of the West Bank and Gaza on the basis that he wanted all Israeli settlements to be removed and refugees to return and receive compensation. He also wanted the Palestinians to be given control over East Jerusalem. The talks ended in failure.

Palestine in the Twenty-first Century

The Palestinian Islamic organisation Hamas emerged during the First Intifada with the objective of liberating Palestine, including Israel, from Israeli occupation and the creation of an Islamic state in the area that is currently Israel, the West Bank and the Gaza Strip. It has consistently launched attacks on Israel with suicide bombings and, since 2001, with rockets. It has also built a network of internal and cross-border tunnels that enable them to transport weapons and bombs for attacks on Israel. Israel tried to destroy this network in a 2014 operation that resulted in the deaths of more than 2,100 people, mostly Palestinians.

Hamas won a large majority in Palestinian elections in 2006, defeating the Fatah party that has links to the Palestinian Liberation Organisation (PLO). When Hamas refused to agree to commit to non-violence, to recognise Israel and to accept previous agreements, the USA, the EU, Russia and the United Nations suspended their aid programmes and Israel imposed economic sanctions. A national unity government was formed to deal with the crisis but, in 2007, rivalry between Fatah and Hamas erupted in violence in the Gaza Strip. This brought the collapse of the Palestinian national unity government and the division of the Palestinian territories into two separate entities; the West Bank, governed by the Palestinian National Authority, and Gaza, controlled by Hamas. Hamas faced an economic blockade by Israel and Egypt. A reconciliation agreement for a joint caretaker Palestinian government was announced in 2011, but it was not until 2014 that an agreement was finally reached to form a unity government until elections could take place.

In 2012, the United Nations upgraded the State of Palestine – as it was now called – to 'non-member observer state' and, as of March 2025, Palestine is recognised as a sovereign state by 147 of the 193 member states of the United Nations, which represents just over 75 per cent of all UN members.

New Threats

Osama bin Laden and the 9/11 Attacks

Few individuals have had as much impact on world history in the last 50 years as Osama bin Laden (1957-2011). Although from humble beginnings and illiterate, his father Mohammed (1908-67) had worked as a freelance contractor during the Saudi Arabian oil boom, becoming chief contractor for public projects in Saudi Arabia. He was a close friend and adviser to the king and was wealthy enough to be able to loan the government money.

Osama bin Laden was radicalised when he was in his mid-teens and became extremely devout, eschewing television, music and western clothes. He was particularly angered by the Israeli-Palestinian situation, dreamt of *jihad* – holy war – and became a member of a local branch of the Muslim Brotherhood. He studied economics at university but most of his time was spent with likeminded radicals, both students and teachers. After dropping out, he went to work in his father's business but when, in 1979, the Soviet Union invaded Afghanistan and resistance there became a matter of *jihad*, Osama bin Laden heeded the call. He travelled to Pakistan and began fundraising for the Afghan *mujahideen*, the guerilla outfits that fought the Russians. He was well connected and one of his campaigns succeeded in raising $100 million. In 1984, he visited Afghanistan for the first time but his trips abroad were causing trouble at home and his brothers fired him from the family firm. He threw himself into the Afghan cause, establishing a base at Peshawar in Pakistan, recruiting Arabs to come and fight and paying all their expenses. Then, in 1986, the Soviets announced their withdrawal from Afghanistan.

Bin Laden linked up with another Islamic militant, Dr. Ayman al-Zawahiri (1951-2022), and in the spring and summer of 1988 they came up with the idea of an international organisation dedicated to *jihad* to be called al-Qaeda (the base). As civil war broke out in Afghanistan following the Soviet withdrawal, bin Laden fought with the *mujahideen* and, when he returned home in late 1989, he was welcomed as a hero. He next turned his attention to another troubled country – South Yemen with its Marxist government. But when the two Yemens, North and South, reunited in the Yemeni Republic, it seemed as if there was little to be done. However, he launched an al-Qaeda campaign of assassinations there, leading the Yemeni government to make an appeal to the Saudi King Fahd as bin Laden was still a Saudi citizen. Eventually, the Saudis confiscated his passport and told him he would be arrested if he continued to encourage violent acts in Yemen.

When the Gulf War broke out, bin Laden tried to dissuade the Saudi Defence Minister from calling on the Americans for help, claiming he could put 100,000 jihadists in the field, but his offer was rejected. After four years back in Peshawar, he began to focus on Sudan where an Islamist government, led by Hasan al-Turabi (1932-2016), had come to power. Bin Laden helped fund and complete some construction projects in Sudan but continued to be disgusted by the American presence in Saudi Arabia, home to Islam's holiest shrines. He funded acts of terrorism perpetrated by his friend al-Zawahiri's Egyptian Islamic Jihad organisation but his funds were beginning to dry up, his family having disowned him. The United States succeeded in forcing Turabi to expel him from Sudan and he went back to Afghanistan where the Taliban leader Mullah Mohammed Omar (c.1950/1962-2013) welcomed him. He set up camp in the caves of the mountainous Tora-Bora region in the east of the country.

Around this time, bin Laden met Khalid Sheikh Mohammed (b. 1964 or 1965), the uncle of Ramzi Yousef (b. 1968) who had tried to blow up the World Trade Center in February 1993. These two had come up with the idea of blowing up a dozen American passenger planes over the Pacific Ocean, an idea that would evolve into the notion of training men to fly planes that could be hijacked and crashed into important American buildings. Meanwhile, bin Laden was becoming famous, and his views were aired on television news programmes and in the press around the world. Following the publication of a fatwa, *al-Quds al-Arabi*, declaring that it was the duty of every devout Muslim to kill Americans, hordes of young jihadists arrived at his base in Afghanistan.

A campaign of outrages began at American embassies in Africa. 213 died in Nairobi, only 12 of whom were Americans, and 11 died in an attack in Tanzania. In October 2000, the USS *Cole* was the victim of a suicide bomber attack in which 17 US sailors died. The American government announced that it suspected al-Qaeda to have been behind the attack. It was an important moment for al-Qaeda and more money came the way of the organisation.

On 11 September 2001, nineteen al-Qaeda members hijacked four commercial airliners on the east coast of the United States, each of the four groups having a pilot in its team. One was flown into the 92nd floor of the New York World Trade Center's North Tower; a second hit the South Tower fifteen minutes later; in Washington, a third plane was crashed into the Pentagon; and the fourth crashed in Pennsylvania after the plane's passengers tried to regain control of the plane. The final death toll for all four events was 2,749. Afterwards, Osama bin Laden claimed responsibility.

Bin Laden became the most wanted person on the planet and President George W. Bush (b. 1946) tried to persuade the Taliban in Afghanistan to hand him over. '... turn over bin Laden or share his fate,' he threatened, and he was as good as his word. On 7 October 2001, the United States launched Operation Enduring Freedom with aerial attacks on the country. A coalition, including troops from the USA, the United Kingdom, Germany, France, Denmark, Australia and Norway arrived in Afghanistan to fight the Taliban. The Northern Alliance, Afghani forces that were opposed to the Taliban, also fought on the coalition's side. They drove the Taliban from power and, in 2004, Hamid Karzai (b. 1957) was elected president of the new Islamic Republic of Afghanistan. Coalition forces remained in the country until 2014 when the United States announced that its combat operations would end.

On 2 May 2011, troops of the United States Navy Sea, Air, Land and Teams group (SEALs) located and killed Osama bin Laden in Abbottabad, Pakistan.

The Iraq War

During the six weeks of the Gulf War, a great deal of Iraq's infrastructure was destroyed. The country was in a poor condition and this was made worse by some of the obligations that the victors placed on Saddam. The country had to pay massive war reparations to Kuwait and recognise Kuwait as an independent nation. Around the world, however, there was great concern about how far Iraq had progressed in the creation of weapons of mass destruction (WMDs), both nuclear and chemical. One of the results of Iraq's defeat, therefore, was that its weapons facilities would have to be opened up to United Nations inspection. In May

1991, the United Nations Special Commission on Disarmament (UNSCOM) began its inspections. Incriminating evidence was uncovered, including weaponised anthrax, large quantities of chemical weapons and signs of a nuclear weapons programme. The United Nations Security Council decided, therefore, to maintain the sanctions it had imposed on Iraq until the country could prove that it was no longer engaged in the production of WMDs. Imports were restricted and anything that could be used in the construction of weapons, such as fertiliser and other types of agricultural equipment, was forbidden. It was crippling for the Iraqi economy. The ban on oil sales meant no foreign exchange and the trade restrictions meant shortages of basic commodities. Saddam, therefore, had little choice but to permit the United Nations officials to carry out the inspections. It was not a smooth process, however, and often weapons material was moved to another location before an inspection, and every possible obstacle was put in front of the inspectors. There would be a series of such situations and, when action was threatened, the Iraqis would climb down and allow the inspectors to do their job.

It was a dreadful time for ordinary Iraqis, unable to access drugs, medicines and food supplies. Infant mortality figures soared and the nation's health system, so buoyed by the oil wealth of the 1970s, was put back half a century. Still, Saddam did not yield an inch and the creation of WMDs remained a higher priority for the government than the well-being of the people it governed. To help the Iraqi people, the UN introduced a scheme whereby Iraq was allowed to sell a limited amount of oil but the proceeds had to be used for the purchase of food and medicine. In 1996, Saddam finally agreed to it.

The UNSCOM inspection teams stopped their inspections in December 1998, having failed to bring Saddam's weapon-making to an end. When they had gone, US and British planes attacked the facilities that the UN officials had been prevented from inspecting but failed to destroy them. Finally, the Iraqis announced that UN inspection teams would not be allowed to return to the country. Meanwhile, in 2000 and 2001, Iraqi anti-aircraft batteries fired on British and US planes patrolling the no-fly zones in the northern and southern regions of the country.

President Bush began pressing for Iraq to cooperate with the United Nations Monitoring, Verification and Inspections Commission (UNMOVIC) that had replaced UNSCOM. He sought the introduction of sanctions targeting military items, but there was resistance in the United Nations. Only Great Britain's Prime Minister Tony Blair (b. 1953) supported the Americans. After the 9/11 attacks, however, things changed; even the Russians amended their position on Iraq. Engaged in their own confrontation with Muslim Chechnyan rebels, they were concerned at the prospect of nuclear weapons falling into the hands of Islamic terrorists. In 2002, President Bush delivered a State of the Union address in which he described an 'Axis of Evil' that included Iraq, Iran and North Korea:

'States like these, and their terrorist allies, constitute an axis of evil, arming to threaten the peace of the world. By seeking weapons of mass destruction, these regimes pose a grave and growing danger. They could provide these arms to terrorists, giving them the means to match their hatred. They could attack our allies or attempt to blackmail the United States. In any of these cases, the price of indifference would be catastrophic. We will work closely with our coalition to deny terrorists and their state sponsors the materials, technology and expertise to make and deliver weapons of mass destruction. We will develop and deploy effective missile defenses to protect America and our allies from sudden attack. And all nations should know: America will do what is necessary to ensure our nation's security.'

In October 2002, President Bush was authorised by the United States Congress to use force against Iraq if necessary and in November, US and British delegates persuaded the United Nations to pass Resolution 1441, proclaiming Iraq to be in 'material breach' of previously passed resolutions. The Iraqi government was called upon to improve its performance. In January 2003, UN inspectors, returning to Iraq, found warheads designed to carry chemical weapons, and surface-to-surface missiles were also discovered. Meanwhile, US Secretary of State Colin Powell (1937-2021) had told the UN Security Council that Iraq was involved in terrorism and was producing WMDs. He made reference to CIA photographs and reports which were later found to be dubious. Finally, President Bush announced: 'Saddam Hussein and his sons must leave Iraq within 48 hours. Their refusal to do so will result in military conflict, commenced at a time of our choosing.' He failed to get the support of the United Nations but, nonetheless, on 19 March, a 'Coalition of the Willing' invaded Iraq. France, Germany and Russia did not take part, but 49 nations did, amongst them Great Britain, Spain, South Korea, Australia and Japan. Three weeks later Coalition forces entered Baghdad, Saddam Hussein having fled. He was later caught, tried and hanged.

Efforts by the United States and its allies to return Iraq to something resembling a civilised country have been fraught with problems and internal warfare remains a problem. In 2009, US forces withdrew from the country although they continue their work there. The insurgency continues with a great deal of crime and violence. In 2013, Sunni militants increased their attacks on Iraq's Shia population, one of their objectives being to show the ineffectiveness of the government of Nouri al-Maliki (b. 1950). Haider al-Abadi (b. 1952) replaced Maliki in 2014, welcomed by the United States as 'another step forward' in bringing Iraq together again. But the violence has continued, and around 600,000 Iraqis have died in factional violence since the invasion. The return of normal basic services has been hindered by this, and it has been reported that the deaths of around 500,000 children can be attributed to malnutrition, disease and other preventable circumstances all linked to the invasion.

The Arab Spring

On 17 December 2010, a 26-year-old Tunisian fruit seller, Mohamed Bouazizi (1984-2011), set himself on fire in protest at the problems and harassment to which he was being subjected in his daily working life. Earlier that day, when he did not have enough money to pay a bribe to the police, he was beaten and his goods were confiscated. Bouazizi's protest and subsequent death sparked a series of nationwide protests against economic stagnation and corruption. The army was eventually called in but refused to fire on the protesters and the president of Tunisia, Zine El Abidine Ben Ali (b. 1936), who had ruled for 23 years, fled the country. It was the beginning of a series of popular uprisings across the Arab world known as the Arab Spring.

By the end of 2011, dictatorships in Egypt, Libya and Yemen had fallen and there were uprisings in Algeria, Iraq, Jordan, Kuwait, Morocco and Sudan as well as other North African and Gulf nations. These protests involved strikes and mass demonstrations with social media employed to disseminate news, organise and communicate. In many places, the response from authorities was violent and, on occasion, this was met with violence from the protesters.

NEW THREATS

In Egypt, protests began on 25 January 2011 and lasted for 18 days. On 28 January, the government attempted to limit internet access to inhibit the ability of the demonstrators to organise and that day President Hosni Mubarak (1928-2020) appointed a new cabinet. Thirteen days later, Mubarak handed presidential power to Vice President Omar Suleiman (1936-2012) but soon afterwards announced that he would be seeing out the remainder of his term as president. As protests continued in Cairo's Tahrir Square, Vice President Suleiman stated that Mubarak had indeed resigned and that his powers had been transferred to the Egyptian armed forces. There was immediate action – the constitution was suspended, parliament was dissolved and the state of emergency that had existed in Egypt for 30 years was rescinded. These actions did not stop the protests, however, which continued as 2011 ended. Mubarak was initially convicted of failing to stop the killings that occurred during the early days of the uprising and sentenced to life in prison but the charges were dismissed in November 2014. He served three years for corruption and died, aged 91, in 2020. Mohamed Morsi (1951-2019) was sworn in as the country's first democratically elected president in 2012 but a year later he was ousted from power by the military.

In Yemen, protests began in January 2011, evolving into a call for the resignation of President Ali Abdullah Saleh (1942-2017) who had been in power for 33 years, the first 12 as president of North Yemen. As the protests continued into February, Saleh announced that he would not seek another term as president in 2013. Protests did not abate with this news, however. In June, when Saleh was injured in an assassination attempt, he was taken to Saudi Arabia for treatment and power was handed over to Vice President Abd Rabbuh Mansur Hadi (b. 1945) who continued with Saleh's policies. In September 2011, Saleh briefly returned to Yemen where, after a great deal of pressure, he finally agreed to step down. In a presidential election in 2012, Hadi was elected president – he was the only candidate. His government was ousted from power in January 2015 by Houthi rebels.

The Houthis took over the presidential palace, installing themselves as the interim government in the form of a Revolutionary Committee headed by Mohammed Ali al-Houthi (b. 1979), a cousin of the Houthi leader, Abdul-Malik al-Houthi (b. 1979). Meanwhile, Hadi, who had travelled to his hometown of Aden, claimed that the Houthi government was unconstitutional and, therefore, invalid. He declared that he was still president and called on government officials and members of Yemen's armed forces to support him.

On 26 March 2015, at the request of Hadi, Saudi Arabia launched a military intervention in Yemen. Heading a coalition of countries from West Asia and North Africa, including Egypt, Morocco, Sudan, Jordan, the United Arab Emirates, Kuwait, Qatar and Bahrain, they launched Operation Decisive Storm, a series of airstrikes on Houthi positions. This was followed by Operation Restoring Hope, a mixture of political, diplomatic and military action with ground forces moving into Yemen to prevent Houthi operations. The Saudi intervention enjoyed the backing of the United States, the United Kingdom, France, Germany and Canada, and the British and Americans provided training for Saudi pilots embarking on air strikes. There was criticism, however, as thousands of civilians lost their lives in the fighting, while the humanitarian crisis in Yemen only got worse as a result of the Saudi action.

By 2019, there was military stalemate and in March 2022, the Saudi coalition announced the cessation of all hostilities in Yemen. Peace talks began, mediated by Oman under the auspices of the United Nations. They continue but have been complicated by the Houthi attacks on shipping in the Red Sea.

NEW THREATS

Syria erupted into protest on 26 January 2011 following the assault of a man by a police officer in Damascus. Demonstrators demanded the release of the assaulted man who had been arrested immediately after the attack. On 6 March, 15 children were arrested in Daraa in the south of the country, charged with writing anti-government graffiti. Protests continued and several died after these escalated following Friday prayers on 18 March. Two days later, when a crowd marched on the Ba'ath Party headquarters and burned them down, security forces fired and shot dead 15 people. Protests were also underway in other parts of the country, calling for the release of political prisoners, the lifting of the state of emergency that had existed for 48 years and an end to corruption in government. On 18 March, there had been protests in a number of major Syrian cities and the authorities responded with tear gas, beatings and water cannon. A week later there were more protests across the country after Friday prayers, at least 70 dying as hundreds of thousands took to the streets. Thousands of activists and protesters were arrested, President Bashar al-Assad (b. 1965) describing them as armed terrorist groups with Islamist extremist motives. He characterised himself as the only means of maintaining a secular government in Syria.

Assad's government began to make compromises in March and April, offering political reforms and changes to its policies. The period of conscription in the Syrian army was reduced and the governor of Daraa was sacked in order to demonstrate that the issue of corruption was being taken seriously. Political prisoners were to be released, taxes cut and more freedom was to be given to Syrian citizens. On 21 April, the state of emergency that had given the government the power to arrest arbitrarily, in order to detain and to prevent political opposition, was lifted. But not many of the reforms actually came to pass. The demonstrations continued.

The Syrian Civil War

The situation in Syria took a turn for the worse when the government started to use troops to try to calm the situation. On 25 April, the Syrian Army moved into the southwestern city of Daraa, arresting hundreds. Live ammunition was used on protesters and water, power and telephone lines were cut off. Hundreds died in clashes and, by 5 May, the army was in control of the city. The same procedure occurred in other towns and cities. As summer approached, the opposition forces became more organised and better equipped, helped also by a number of senior military or security personnel who defected to their side. In Jisr al-Shughur, close to the Turkish border, as armed clashes erupted between protesters and security forces, 10,000 residents of the town, fearing they would be massacred, fled across the border into Turkey. Aleppo saw large protests in early July and, on 3 July, tanks were deployed in Hama. On 29 July, the founding of the Free Syrian Army was announced by some of the officers who had crossed over to the opposition side, its objective to unseat Bashar al-Assad. They also created the Syrian National Council which later united with other opposition groups to form the National Coalition for Syrian Revolutionary and Opposition Forces. The coalition was recognised by many countries as the legitimate representative of the Syrian people.

The violence continued even after former UN Secretary General Kofi Annan (1938-2018) drafted a peace plan, and there was outrage around the world in 2012 when the Syrian government was found to be using heavy weaponry against its own citizens and when it was learned that 100 civilians had been massacred by the army in Houla, near the city of Homs. The death toll during the first six months of the insurgency numbered around 11,000 and the United Nations has estimated that around 1.2 million Syrians were displaced in the early stages of the fighting, some 355,000 fleeing to neighbouring Jordan, Iraq, Lebanon and Turkey.

Both sides have been accused of human rights violations but it is difficult to verify these and now the conflict can be viewed as a sectarian one. The Syrian government is, generally, of the Shia Alawite persuasion and it is opposed by mainly Sunni Muslims on the rebel side. Christians, Druze and Armenians have sided with the government while Turkmen have taken up the rebel cause. Kurds and Palestinians seem undecided, the Kurds having fought on both sides. Minority Christians have been targeted and all 50,000 Christians in Homs have left the city.

Sanctions were applied against the Syrian government by the United States, the European Union, the Organisation of Islamic Cooperation and the Gulf Cooperation Council but, by the end of 2012, there appeared to be a stalemate, the rebels holding northern areas but restricted by poor weaponry and organisation. The civilian death toll continued to climb as fighting took place in the contested areas. Other countries began supplying arms to both sides, the rebels funded and armed by Turkey, Saudi Arabia and Qatar while the Syrian government was receiving weapons from Iran and the Lebanese militant organisation, Hezbollah. Hezbollah fighters were also sent into battle.

Calls for international military action were heightened by a suspected chemical weapons attacks in Damascus, allegedly by the forces supporting the president. This was denied, the Syrian government blaming the other side for the attacks. The major powers started to indicate that they might entertain the idea of retaliatory strikes against the Assad regime, but it was evident in the United States and Great Britain, at least, that such strikes would be unpopular with the electorate. Meanwhile, President Assad agreed to the removal or destruction of Syria's chemical weapons.

The Syrian rebels established the Syrian Interim Government after seizing the regional capitals of Raqqa and Idlib in 2013 and 2015 respectively. Meanwhile, pro-Assad forces were receiving military and financial support from Iran and Russia, Iran having been involved in the civil war since 2013. At Assad's request, Russia launched an intervention in 2015, claiming to be acting against what it described as 'terrorism'. This intervention consisted of extensive air strikes across Syria, ostensibly aimed at ISIS but, in reality, hitting sites used by the Free Syrian Army, the Revolutionary Command Council — an alliance of 72 rebel factions — as well as Sunni militant groups that had joined together to form the Army of Conquest. Russian forces deployed to Syria included special operations troops, military advisers and private military contractors such as the Wagner Group which was funded by the Russian state and led until 2023 by Yevgeny Prigozhin (1961-2023), at the time a close ally of the Russian president, Vladimir Putin (b. 1952).

In September 2016, a ceasefire that had been negotiated between Russia, Syria and rebel forces backed by the West broke down and Syrian government forces began bombing the eastern part of the Aleppo region. There were many civilian casualties as medical facilities and aid workers were targeted using cluster bombs and incendiary bombs. The world was again outraged but the bombing continued until Aleppo was seized in December 2016.

Meanwhile, ISIS was struggling as it fought on three fronts — against US-supported Kurdish forces, pro-Assad forces enjoying the support of Iran and Russia and a coalition of rebel groups that had the backing of Turkey. The organisation lost strategically vital territories along the Turkish border to Kurdish troops and forces supported by Turkey while its bases were being hammered by an air campaign led by the United States. In Idlib, it was losing ground to a coalition known as Hayat Tahrir al-Sham (HTS) which included ISIS's great ideological rivals, the al-Nusra Front. June 2017 saw ISIS defeated by Kurdish Syrian Democratic forces at Raqqa, at that point ISIS's principal stronghold in Syria and in the east. Five months later Assad's forces pushed them out of the city of Deir ez-Zour. Around this time, HTS created the Syrian Salvation Government to govern Idlib, gaining useful experience of government that would serve it well after the 2024 ousting of Bashar al-Assad.

Western nations became increasingly involved in the conflict. Following another chemical attack – in Khān Shaykhūn – in April 2017, the United States Air Force unleashed 59 Tomahawk missiles on the Shayrat airbase. A year later, following another chemical attack in Douma, dozens of strikes were carried out by British and French planes on facilities producing chemical weapons near Homs and Damascus. Israel became involved in 2018, attacking Iranian forces in Syria. Iran responded by shelling the Golan Heights, Israel replying with the heaviest barrage of missiles since the start of the civil war, targeting numerous Iranian bases.

By June 2018, Syrian government forces had secured the areas around Damascus and Homs. They next began to retake areas in Daraa, in the southwest of the country, that had been captured by rebels who were given safe passage northwards to Idlib in return for their surrender. The focus now fell on Idlib, the last remaining rebel stronghold. However, Turkish troops massed along the border in support of the rebels, faced by troops of the Syrian government. Meanwhile, border towns were bombed by Syrian and Russian jets. In order to bring some calm to the situation, the Russians and the Turkish established a buffer zone about 15 to 20 kilometres wide between the opposing forces. In the agreement for the buffer zone, Turkey had agreed to rein in the HTS but, in January 2019, the HTS launched an offensive against other rebel groups in the area, establishing itself as the dominant force in Idlib. In April, ignoring the buffer zone, Syrian forces launched an offensive in Idlib with air support provided by the Russians. In June, they were pushed back but the fighting spread to the east in October when Turkey attacked the northeast of Syria, an area held by Kurdish forces, the United States having indicated that they would not intervene in this action. The Kurds reached a deal with Assad for assistance and for the first time in eight years, government forces entered the region.

After a period of calm, a new rebel offensive was launched in 2024. By this time, Russia was preoccupied with its invasion of Ukraine and Iran's focus was on the Israel-Hamas War. International support for the Syrian government was, therefore, much less than before. Furthermore, Hezbollah – vital to Assad in his fight against the rebel forces – was severely damaged by Israeli bombing of Lebanon between September and November. Forced to defend against invasion, Hezbollah withdrew its troops from Syria. A ceasefire deal between Hezbollah and Israel was agreed towards the end of November but it left Hezbollah without the resources to fight outside Lebanon.

On 27 November 2024, HTS began to advance in the provinces of Idlib and Aleppo, taking the latter city two days later. They reached Ham in the next few days and, on 7 December, Daraa and Homs were taken, effectively cutting Damascus off from military supplies. Within a day, the capital had fallen but there was no sign of Bashar al-Assad who had fled, it was believed, to Moscow.

It was announced on 10 December 2024 that, until March 2025, Mohammed al-Bashir (b. 1983), head of the Syrian Salvation Government in Idlib, would fulfil the role of interim prime minister. In January 2025, Ahmed al-Sharaa (b. 1982), who was leader of the HTS, was declared interim president. In early March, with no certainties surrounding elections or a new constitution, interim government loyalists acted against Assad supporters in the predominantly Alawite parts of western Syria. In just four days, more than 1,000 civilians lost their lives at the hands of government forces.

The Kurds came onside when they reached an agreement with the interim government whereby Kurds would become equal citizens of the new Syria. Around this time, the Kurdistan Workers' Party (PKK) declared a ceasefire with the Turkish government.

Although the head of the transitional government, Prime Minister al-Bashir, has stated that Christians and other minorities would be free to practise their religion, many are dubious that this will actually happen. These doubts arise from the fact that many in the rebel forces have been connected at some point to al-Qaeda and Islamic State. The fear is, therefore, that the new state of Syria may turn out to be less secular than hoped.

Afghanistan

Before becoming a presidential candidate in June 2015, Donald Trump (b. 1946) had been calling for a speedy exit from Afghanistan, declaring the American effort there to be a huge waste of US 'blood and treasure' and tweeting 'Let's get out!' After becoming president of the United States in 2016, however, rather than withdraw, he renewed the US commitment to the 16-year-long war, announcing that he was now of the opinion that to pull out could create a vacuum that would be filled by terrorists such as al-Qaeda and Islamic State. He would not be drawn on the numbers of troops it would take but insisted that they must 'fight to win'.

The fighting in the country had begun in 2001 with the US launch of Operation Enduring Freedom following the devastating September 11 attacks on the World Trade Center in New York

City. The United Kingdom and United States joint combat operation ended on 26 October 2014 and in December that year, NATO ended its combat operations. Military operations continued, carried out by private security companies engaged by the United Nations and the US government.

Around this time, encouraged by the withdrawal of foreign troops, the Taliban were making a comeback. Their ranks were bolstered by the arrival of thousands of Uzbek, Arab and Pakistani militants pushed out of North Waziristan by the Pakistani military. Meanwhile, the international community was increasingly turning its attention away from Afghanistan to other trouble spots such as Ukraine, Yemen, Syria and Iraq. The Taliban were further encouraged by the lack of resources and the failings of the Afghan military and by the weakness of the government in Kabul. They governed in the areas they had captured from government troops and established a reputation for dispensing a less corrupt form of justice than could be obtained from the country's law courts. They continued to make progress in the country and, by July 2016, *Time* magazine was reporting that at least 20 per cent of Afghanistan was under Taliban control. By January 2017, 33 districts, spread across 16 provinces were controlled by them while the government retained control of 258. The struggle for the remaining 120 was ongoing. Meanwhile, the American presence in the country was raised to 14,000 troops.

In January 2018, the Taliban were continuing to establish a grip on parts of Afghanistan and Islamic State was becoming increasingly involved in the struggle for the country. The continuing violence of their attacks persuaded President Trump and the Afghan government to rule out any notion of peace talks with the insurgents, although this changed towards the end of February when the Afghan president, Ashraf Ghani (b. 1949), proposed holding unconditional peace talks with them. He suggested that they could be recognised as a legitimate political party and that Taliban prisoners could be released, responding to Afghans' desire for a negotiated end to the war that had been tearing their country apart for so long. There was no response, however, from the Taliban. Following large demonstrations, sit-in protests and marches by disgruntled Afghans, Ghani and the Taliban agreed a ceasefire to take place during the celebrations for the important Islamic festival, Eid al-Fitr, in June. When the ceasefire ended, however, on 18 June, the Taliban went back to war but talks between the various parties carried on for the rest of the year.

Fighting continued through 2019, with an attempt at peace negotiations between the United States and the Taliban collapsing in September that year. Finally, on 29 February 2020, a conditional peace deal was signed in Doha between the Taliban and the United States. A prisoner exchange was to happen within 10 days and all US troops were to be withdrawn from Afghanistan within 14 months. The Taliban had consistently refused to permit the Afghan government to be involved in the talks, viewing it as little more than a puppet for the Americans and, naturally, President Ghani opposed the idea. He insisted that his government had never agreed to release 5,000 Taliban captives, that it was a decision for his government to make, not the United States. Despite the agreement, the fighting carried on and the United States responded to Taliban attacks in the provinces of Helmand and Kunduz with an air strike.

By August 2020, just over 5,000 prisoners had been released by the Afghan government while the Taliban had released 1,000 captives. By March 2021, peace talks were taking place between Ghani and the Taliban. They discussed holding elections for a democratically elected government. A month later, US President Joe Biden (b. 1942) announced that the last 2,500 American troops would be withdrawn from Afghanistan by 11 September, the twentieth anniversary of the 9/11 attacks. On 1 May, meanwhile, the Taliban mounted their last offensive, capturing Kabul without any resistance on 15 August. President Ghani fled to Tajikistan as the Taliban swept into the Arg, the Afghan presidential palace. They declared the war to be over.

In the next two weeks there was a mad dash to evacuate people who would be in danger following the Taliban takeover – interpreters and others who had worked with the coalition forces, as well as ethnic minorities. Day after day, foreign diplomatic staff, military and civilian staff and Afghan citizens were airlifted out of Hamid Karzai International Airport, and the US military switched its attention from attacking Taliban positions to providing security for the airport. The US campaign in Afghanistan – America's longest war – ended on 30 August when the last plane took off.

At the head of the Taliban government is supreme leader Hibatullah Akhundzada (b. 1961), and Hasan Akhund (b. 1945), one of the four Taliban founders, is prime minister. As a result of the Taliban takeover, western nations and many organisations – including the World Bank and the International Monetary Fund (IMF) – withdrew funding for the country, resulting in an economic and banking crisis and a widespread shortage of food. However, since the Taliban takeover, Afghanistan has moved up the Corruption Perceptions Index from position 174 to 150, although in 2023, it dropped 12 places. This was a result of the government's focus on tackling bribery and corruption. By contrast, the situation regarding human rights has worsened. Restrictions on women and girls have increased, and women have been banned from appearing in public alone or travelling more than 72 kilometres without a male chaperone. Girls have been banned from education beyond primary school and gender-based violence has increased. Freedom of expression has also suffered, and criticism of the Taliban can result in enforced disappearance, unlawful detention, arbitrary arrest and torture. Ethnic groups, including religious minorities, have been increasingly marginalised and face prejudice. Public executions have been reintroduced and punishments such as stoning and flogging have become common.

Iran

The veteran politician and cleric, Hassan Rouhani, who replaced Mahmoud Ahmadinejad as Iranian president in 2013, was considered a moderate conservative. The margin of his victory – winning more than 50 per cent of the first-round vote and thus negating the need for a second round – could be interpreted as a desire by the country to turn away from the hard-line approach taken by his predecessor. That approach, many Iranians believed, had led to increasing isolation for their country as well as an ailing economy.

By reintegrating his erstwhile shunned nation into the global economy once more, a consequence of the signature of an agreement limiting its nuclear programme, Rouhani succeeded in stabilising the Iranian economy, making inflation manageable and producing signs of growth. During his election campaign, he had committed to the resumption of international negotiations in order to reduce sanctions on Iran and when he took office he launched diplomatic efforts to improve relations between Iran and the West. In November 2013, negotiations began between Iran, China, France, the United Kingdom and the United States, and, by December, an interim agreement had been reached which reduced sanctions on Iran in exchange for a cutback on the country's nuclear development. After eight days of complex discussion, a framework was finally established in April 2015 that provided more detail. Iran would hand over 98 per cent of its highly enriched uranium. Further enrichment and nuclear research would be restricted and subject to monitoring by the International Atomic Energy Agency. The Joint Comprehensive Plan of Action was reached in July 2015 and January 2016 brought the lifting of international economic sanctions.

In the presidential election in 2017, Rouhani – campaigning on a more reformist agenda – won by a landslide, taking 57 per cent of the vote, his nearest rival, the conservative cleric, Ebrahim Raisi (1960-2024), managing only 38 per cent. As time passed, however, it became clear that Iran's new wealth, achieved mostly in the oil sector, was not trickling down to ordinary people. Certainly, Gross Domestic Product (GDP) had risen sharply, and inflation was lower than it had been for many years, but the unemployment rate remained in double figures. This dissatisfaction led to huge demonstrations and protests in December 2017.

During his 2015 campaign for the US presidency, Donald Trump had said repeatedly that he would withdraw America from the Iran nuclear deal, and in May 2018, he did just that. Sanctions returned the following November in an effort to force Iran to withhold support for militant groups in the region and to stop its development of ballistic missiles. Of course, when the United States withdrew from the agreement, the Iranian GDP went down, and the inflation rate reached its highest point in decades.

In February 2020, in the midst of economic turmoil, and with the relationship with the United States at a low ebb, Iranians went to the polls to elect a new Majlis, the Iranian parliament. It was a foregone conclusion that the results would favour the Supreme Leader, Ali Khamenei, especially as almost 7,000 candidates were disqualified, including 90 sitting members of the Majlis, most of them centrists or reformists. With the lowest voter turnout since the revolution in 1979 – probably due to COVID-19 which had broken out in Iran two days before the election – the conservatives recorded the expected resounding victory.

The turnout for the 2021 presidential election was not much better, once again below 50 per cent. This time, however, the low turnout was probably due to apathy rather than anything else. In this election Rouhani could not stand due to the limit on the number of terms a president could serve. It was also likely that, as a reformist, he would not have been allowed to stand anyway. With little opposition, Ebrahim Raisi won with a huge majority.

As expected, he surrounded himself with like-minded hardliners who would champion the policies of the Supreme Leader, Khamenei. As inflation continued to rise and people suffered real hardship, little was done to alleviate the situation. Nonetheless, funds were still found for the Revolutionary Guards, the branch of the military that protects the Islamic Republic. It seemed that, despite his protests that he was going to deal with the failing economy, all Raisi was interested in was securing the future of the regime. Meanwhile, negotiations to lift sanctions once again were faltering and the problems caused to the global economy by the Russian invasion of Ukraine did not help the situation.

There were protests across Iran when prices of some foods tripled after Khamenei cut the subsidies on them. More demonstrations followed the suspicious death in custody of a young Kurdish woman, Mahsa Amini, her 'crime' being that she failed to wear the hijab in accordance with government standards. The authorities claimed that she had a heart attack at a police station and fell into a coma but eyewitnesses contradicted this version of events, claiming that she died as a result of a severe beating by police officers. The incident brought home to many the injustices of the Iranian regime, especially towards women and, indeed, women were at the forefront of the protest movement. They took off their veils and even cut their hair in public. A chant that had been used by Kurds rang out at demonstrations – '*Zan! Zendegī! Āzādī!*' ('Women! Life! Freedom!'). Protest spread through Iranian society and there were hopes that the requirement for the head covering might be rescinded. These were dashed, however, and the authorities continued to enforce the wearing of the hijab.

In May 2024, Raisi was killed when a helicopter in which he was travelling crashed near the village of Uzi in East Azerbaijan province after a visit to Azerbaijan. Two months later, Masoud Pezeshkian (b. 1954) was elected president of Iran.

Hezbollah and Lebanon

In November 2017, while visiting Saudi Arabia, Lebanese prime minister, Saad al-Hariri (b. 1970), unexpectedly announced in a recorded address that was critical of Iran and Hezbollah that he was resigning. It was immediately suspected that Hariri was being held against his will by the Saudi authorities and had been strong-armed into resigning, suspicions that were later confirmed. Western and Arab leaders put pressure on the Saudi government to release him and he was freed in late November, swiftly withdrawing his resignation. Hariri was not forthcoming about why he was held by the Saudis, and neither were his captors, although it is suspected that Saudi prime minister, Prince Mohammed bin Salman (b. 1985), was frustrated by Hariri's soft-pedalling with Hezbollah.

In the 2018 legislative election, Hariri's March 14 bloc of political parties lost its majority, and victory went to the March 8 bloc which was led by Hezbollah. Nonetheless, Hariri was prime minister designate but the process of forming a government acceptable to all parties was fraught with difficulty. The machinations dragged on into 2019, made all the more urgent by gathering problems, including a growing debt crisis that was exacerbated by the lack of a functioning government. Confidence in the country's economy plummeted. To make matters worse, the Israelis uncovered tunnels that crossed the border from Lebanon and claimed that they had been dug by Hezbollah to be used in a planned future attack. Worries grew that Israel might enter Lebanon while the country was still rudderless. Finally, on 30 January 2019, a national unity government was formed, the cabinet featuring representation from most parties and including four women ministers. Hezbollah wielded great influence in this new regime but maintained a low profile in some areas as their presence might endanger vital funding.

In October 2019, as unrest grew over corruption, the state of the economy and a new internet tax, massive protests erupted across the country. The situation had been made worse a few days prior to the protests by a series of wildfires that created a wildlife disaster and rendered thousands of people homeless. The government's response was less than satisfactory. Firefighting equipment was found to be faulty, and poorly maintained. Funds for its maintenance had been stolen over the years. In the face of a surge of anti-government feeling, the internet tax was cancelled, and an emergency reform package was hastily put together, although it was not enough to bring the protests and demands for resignations to a halt. Finally, Hariri resigned on 29 October 2019, this time for real. Despite further protests and the refusal of Hariri's March 14 bloc to work with him, Lebanese academic, engineer and politician, Hassan Diab (b. 1959), was named as Lebanon's new premier on 21 January 2020. He assembled a cabinet of technocrats and political outsiders, but questions were asked about their competence and whether they were truly independent of the existing political parties.

As COVID-19 began to rage across the world, the Lebanese pound collapsed, resulting in the country defaulting on its debts. As a result, Lebanese banks placed a limit on how much depositors could withdraw, and restrictions were also introduced on the transfer of money abroad, capital controls that it was anticipated would remain in place until 2025, at the earliest. Months of lockdowns due to the pandemic did not help but to provide a boost for the economy, the government made cannabis production legal. It also started negotiations with the International Monetary Fund for a bail-out but these collapsed in July and this led to a period of hyperinflation. To make matters even worse, on 4 August 2020, there was a major explosion in Beirut, the Lebanese capital. More than 2,700 tonnes of negligently stored ammonium nitrate, a chemical used predominantly in agriculture, exploded in a massive mushroom cloud near the port. There were 218 deaths, 7,000 people were injured and a huge amount of damage, estimated to be around $15 billion, was done to the surrounding area. Around 300,000 people were displaced, and 90 per cent of the city's hotels were damaged. The anti-government protests increased in ferocity and, six days after the explosion, after a state of emergency had been declared, Hassan Diab and his government resigned.

As usual in Lebanon, finding a new government proved difficult, even after pressure from the French president, Emmanuel Macron (b. 1977), whose country was providing aid following the explosion. It took a year for Najib Mikati (b. 1955) to be named prime minister in September 2021. Elections in May 2022 saw the Hezbollah faction lose its majority but Mikati remained in his post as prime minister.

Tensions along the Israel-Lebanon border, growing out of a disagreement over the extraction of natural gas from a disputed maritime area, led to confrontations between the two states, especially after Hamas's October 2023 attacks on Israeli civilians close to the Gaza Strip. Targeted strikes by the Israelis in 2023 killed a number of Hezbollah commanders in Lebanon. Then, in September 2024, thousands of Hezbollah pagers and walkie-talkies exploded killing dozens and injuring thousands. A few days later, Israel launched attacks in southern Lebanon and Beirut, ostensibly targeting Hezbollah bases but killing hundreds, including many civilians. On 25 September, a Hezbollah missile, heading for Tel Aviv – the first time Hezbollah had targeted Israel in this way – was destroyed by Israeli defences. Two days later, Israeli bombs fell on Dahieh, south of Beirut, killing Hezbollah leader, Hassan Nasrallah (1960-2024). The Israelis finally invaded southern Lebanon on 1 October, resulting in widespread destruction in the region. A ceasefire agreement was reached on 26 November.

A new Lebanese president, Joseph Aoun (b. 1964), was appointed in January 2025. Widely trusted both at home and abroad, he promised at his inauguration to impose state control over the possession of arms in his country and to secure southern Lebanon.

The Rise of Islamic State

The self-proclaimed caliphate, Islamic State of Iraq and the Levant (ISIL), is also known as the Islamic State of Iraq and Syria (ISIS), the Islamic State of Iraq and as-Sham and Dawlat al-Islamiyah f'al-Iraq w Belaad al-Sham (Daesh). It is an extremist militant group led by and mainly consisting of Sunni Arabs from Iraq and Syria, its self-styled status as a caliphate allowing it to lay claim to religious, military and political authority over all the world's Muslims.

It was founded by the Jordanian militant Islamist Abu Musab al-Zarqawi (1966-2006) in 1999 and made a name for itself in the Iraq insurgency for its suicide bomb attacks on Shia mosques. In 2004, it pledged allegiance to al-Qaeda, continuing its attacks on security forces, civilians, foreign diplomats and soldiers. On 7 June 2006, al-Zarqawi was killed in a drone attack and was succeeded by the Egyptian radical, Abu Ayyub al-Masri (1968-2010). The United States reckoned in 2007 that al-Qaeda in Iraq (AQI), one of the names it used at the time, was planning to create a Sunni caliphate in central and western Iraq. US troops eliminated a number of high-ranking AQI members that year and in the next year it suffered a number of defeats and declined in power. In 2010, al-Masri was killed along with another senior organisation figure, Abu Omar Baghdadi (?-2010), by US forces. At the time it was reported by a US general that around 80 per cent of the Islamic State in Iraq's leaders had been killed. The Iraqi Abu Bakr al-Baghdadi (1971-2019) — a man with a $10 million reward on his head — took over.

Following the outbreak of the Syrian Civil War, Baghdadi began sending Islamic State of Iraq members to establish the organisation there. It became known as Jabhat al-Nusra (al-Nusra Front) and rapidly became an important force for those who were opposed to Syrian President Assad. At this point there was some confusion as Baghdadi released a statement announcing the merger of ISI and the al-Nusra Front but the latter organisation's leader, Abu Muhammad al-Julani (b. 1974 or 1981), said he knew nothing about any merger. The Arabic television station Al Jazeera released a letter by the al-Qaeda leader Ayman al-Zawahiri in which he disapproved of such a merger but al-Baghdadi announced that, despite this, the merger was happening. This internal struggle continued for some time until eventually al-Qaeda announced that it had split with the Islamic State of Iraq and the Levant, as ISI was now known. Al-Nusra carries on its fight to depose Assad but ISIL is more focused on conquering territory in order to create an Islamic state, attacking other sectarian groups and imposing Shariah law as soon as it has taken over an area. Meanwhile, a series of gruesome beheadings of kidnapped Westerners by ISIL horrified and disgusted the world.

On 29 June 2014, ISIL proclaimed itself a worldwide caliphate with Abu Bakr al-Baghdadi as caliph. The fighting in both Iraq and Syria continues and in October 2014 ISIL fighters were reported to have advanced to within 16 miles of Baghdad Airport. Their war has now stretched into Libya with the capture in 2014 of the Libyan city of Derna. Other militant groups such as the Egyptian Ansar Bait al-Maqdis and the Nigerian Boko Haram have sworn allegiance to ISIL and recruitment takes place across the Arab world and elsewhere. Airstrikes by a US-led coalition began in August 2014, an initiative described by President Barack Obama (b. 1961) as a 'long-term project'. By July 2015, the Coalition had flown more than 44,000 sorties against ISIL.

The Refugee Crisis

The fighting and disruption in the Middle East, as well as ISIL's growing stranglehold on many parts of the region led, in 2015, to a tidal wave of refugees seeking asylum in Europe. An estimated 1.3 million people arrived, 71 per cent of them originating in Syria, Eritrea and Afghanistan, according to the United Nations High Commissioner for Refugees. The danger of the crossings and the subsequent tragic deaths caused consternation in Europe, but European Union states received 626,000 applications for asylum in 2014, the highest number of applications since 1992.

Syria was, without doubt, the biggest contributor to this huge movement of people. There, civilians were being brutally attacked by both sides in the ongoing civil war. As we have seen, President Assad's regime used chemical weapons and barrel bombs against them, while ISIS employed barbaric practices such as crucifixion, practised sexual slavery and committed many atrocities in the country. Other groups such as al-Nusra also indulged in horrific acts against civilians. Most Syrian refugees ended up in crowded and often dangerous camps in neighbouring countries and to escape this hopeless situation, many embarked on the perilous journey across the Mediterranean to Europe, often entrusting themselves and their families to unscrupulous human traffickers.

In summer 2015, the European Union, the United States and Kuwait respectively promised $1.2 billion, $507 million and $500 million to alleviate the refugee problem but this was far from sufficient. The richer countries of the West refused to help fund policies that would make the refugees' journey less dangerous, believing that the inherent danger would dissuade people from embarking on the journey. Great Britain, for instance, cut funding for Italy's Mare Nostrum search-and-rescue project that is estimated to have saved the lives of many thousands of people. That initiative was replaced by the European Union's much less effective Frontex programme, Operation Triton, that patrols only within 30 miles of the border and does not have the search-and-rescue impetus.

Once in Europe, the refugees' journey got no easier. Hungary, for instance, erected a razor-wire fence along its border with Serbia to stop them entering the country and arrested any who did. Austria introduced checks along its borders, a violation, many claimed, of Europe's policy of open borders as specified in the Schengen Agreement, and numerous EU member states also reacted by closing their borders. Germany did most to accommodate the asylum seekers, receiving more than 440,000 applications. Hungary took in 174,000, Sweden 156,000 and Austria 88,000. Of course, many in these countries opposed this, citing the difficulties of integrating migrants and the cultural challenges inherent in doing so. Immigration emerged as a hot political topic and brought a surge in the popularity of right-wing populist parties across the continent.

With the ongoing instability of the Middle East, the refugee crisis continued. Syrian refugees have sought asylum in more than 130 countries, the majority – around 5 million – in neighbouring countries such as Turkey, Lebanon, Jordan, Iran and Egypt. With the fall of the Assad government in December 2024, however, more than a million Syrians returned home, 301,967 from Turkey, Lebanon and Jordan, while 885,294 internally displaced persons also returned to their homes. In April 2024, a regional survey by the United Nations Humanitarian Relief agency reported that 57 per cent of Syrian refugees said that they hoped to return home, but with the fall of Assad that number increased to more than 80 per cent. Spontaneous returns are forecast to continue throughout 2025.

Meanwhile, in Syria there is widespread poverty and unemployment, more than 90 per cent of the population living below the poverty line. The economic crisis has rendered around 12.9 million people food insecure. It is little better for refugees living in neighbouring territories. Countries such as Lebanon have their own economic challenges and more than 90 per cent of Syrians living there are reliant on humanitarian aid. In Jordan, it is estimated that more than 93 per cent of Syrian refugees have gone into debt to be able to afford their basic needs. The situation is the same in Turkey. This dire state of affairs, of course, opens up the possibility of protection risks such as child labour, gender-based violence and child marriage, amongst other forms of exploitation. Agencies such as UNHCR are working to alleviate the situation, providing homes, schools and recreation centres, as well as educational activities for children and psycho-social support.

Israel and the Gaza War

In July 2014, in response to an escalation in rocket attacks by Hamas, Israel launched Operation Protective Edge in the Gaza Strip, the Palestinian territory governed by Hamas since 2007. This incursion by ground troops was aimed at stopping the rockets fired by Hamas and destroying Hamas's cross-border tunnels. The conflict lasted just seven weeks but it was one of the deadliest in decades between the two bitter enemies, more than 2,000 people – mainly Gazan Palestinians – losing their lives.

The invasion by Israeli ground forces ended on 5 August leading to the declaration of an open-ended ceasefire on 26 August. The Israeli Defence Force (IDF) announced that during the conflict, Hamas, Palestinian Islamic Jihad (PIJ) and other Palestinian militant factions, had unleashed 4,564 rockets and mortars into Israeli territory, and 735 of them had been shot down or destroyed by Iron Dome, Israel's mobile, all-weather air defence system. Five thousand, two hundred and sixty-three targets were hit by the IDF and at least thirty-four of the Hamas-built tunnels under the border were destroyed. More than 2,000 Gazans died in the conflict and at least 10,000 were injured, including 3,374 children. Sixty-seven IDF soldiers and five Israeli civilians lost their lives.

As a result of the fighting, Gazan hospitals suffered severe shortages of medicine, medical equipment and fuel and, to help the situation, the IDF set up a field hospital for Gazans at the Erez Crossing. In addition, the vital Rafah Crossing between Egypt and Gaza was reopened by the Egyptians to allow much-needed supplies to get through. By this time, 83,000 Palestinians were being looked after by the United Nations in refugee camps but the Palestinian nationalist and social democratic political party, Fatah, accused Hamas of stealing the aid that had been sent and distributing it to members of Hamas, or even of selling it on the black market. More than 273,000 Palestinians were displaced, and hundreds of homes were destroyed or badly damaged.

In Israel, meanwhile, elections were held on 17 March 2015 after serious disagreements in November and December 2014 amongst the governing coalition over the budget and the 'Jewish state' proposal, an Israeli law that specifies the country's significance to the Jewish people. Criticised internationally this law was viewed by many to be racist and undemocratic. As a result of the election, Benjamin Netanyahu (b. 1949) retained the premiership and, by the 6 May deadline, had formed a coalition with the Jewish Home, United Torah Judaism, Kulanu and Shas parties, all right-leaning groups.

In December 2017, US President Donald Trump announced that the United States formally recognised Jerusalem to be the capital of Israel and, in March the following year, announced recognition of the Golan Heights as part of Israel, making the USA the first country to do so. Two-thirds of that area had been occupied by Israel following the Six-Day War of 1967 and had been, effectively, annexed in 1981, an act that had remained unrecognised by the rest of the world which considered it to be Syrian territory that was occupied by Israel.

Netanyahu's premiership came under threat in February 2018 when criminal corruption charges were made against him, a police statement saying that there was sufficient evidence to indict him of bribery, fraud and breach of trust. He maintained that the charges were groundless and insisted on continuing in his role as prime minister. On 28 January 2020, he was officially charged with three counts of bribery and corruption, the first sitting prime minister in Israeli history to be charged with a crime.

One charge alleged that Netanyahu had traded political favours for gifts such as expensive cigars, jewellery and champagne while another alleged that he had tried to obtain favourable coverage from the Israeli newspaper, *Yedioth Ahronoth*, in return for cutting the circulation of a rival newspaper, *Israel Hayom*. Charges were also laid against people from the prime minister's inner circle in a third case which alleged bribery in Isarel's purchase of submarines from the German company, ThyssenKrupp. A further case alleged that Netanyahu had enabled favourable regulatory policies for a telecommunications company, Bezeq, in return for positive media coverage. The prime minister again denied all the charges and once again refused to resign. His partners in the ruling coalition began to abandon him, however, mainly due to disagreements about policies. Eventually, he lost control of the Knesset and elections were called for April 2019.

Six weeks before that date, the Israeli attorney general announced that he would be pursuing the charges against Netanyahu but, in spite of that, his party, Likud, performed well in the elections. He still failed to obtain the number of seats necessary to form a government, however, and there were problems forming a coalition, mainly caused by disagreements about the conscription of male followers of Haredi Judaism, a strict branch of Orthodox Judaism. A September election also provided no coalition. In an attempt to break the stalemate, a third election was staged in March 2020 but again Netanyahu failed to put together a coalition. Instead, Benny Gantz (b. 1959), a retired army general of the National Unity faction in the Knesset, was given a mandate to form a government. Around this time, however, COVID-19 began to rage across Israel and Gantz agreed to the formation of an emergency unity government with Benjamin Netanyahu as prime minister. An agreement was arrived at whereby Netanyahu would hand the premiership to Gantz in 18 months.

The unity government, severely criticised for how it handled the COVID-19 crisis, did not last long and with Netanyahu's trial for corruption now underway, his popularity was at an all-time low in the country. This was despite the Abraham Accords, a set of agreements mediated by the United States through which several Arab countries agreed to normalise their relationships with Israel. But problems remained at home and when the government was unable to pass the 2021 budget, the Knesset was dissolved for elections to be held in March 2021. Yet again, Netanyahu failed to win the necessary majority and Naftali Bennett (b. 1972), leader of the New Right party, became prime minister of Israel.

Netanyahu's trial was coming under close scrutiny at this time and it was revealed that the police had hacked the phones of some witnesses, leading to public distrust of the whole legal process. The credibility of the trial was also damaged when the prime minister's defence team proved that a meeting important to the case could not have taken place on the date specified in the indictment.

By this time, Netanyahu was encouraging members of the coalition to defect to the opposition in order to bring down Bennett's government. Eventually, in June, after Netanyahu had ordered the members of the Knesset loyal to him to vote against the renewal of an emergency regulation that had, since 1967, ensured that Israeli settlements in the West Bank were governed by civil authorities rather than military, Bennett's government collapsed. He announced the dissolution of the Knesset with elections to be held in November.

Netanyahu was returned to office as part of a coalition that included ministers with far-right tendencies. One cabinet minister was even prevented from taking the job by the Israeli High Court of Justice because at the time he was serving a suspended sentence. This only encouraged Netanyahu in his views that the judiciary should be subject to more government control which, of course, could have implications for his corruption trial. His attempts at reform led to widespread strikes and protests by Israelis. By August 2023, senior military officials were issuing warnings that the Israeli Defence Forces were unprepared for war.

As if to confirm this accusation, on 7 October 2023, Hamas launched a deadly attack on Israel by land, sea and air, a meticulously planned operation in which around 1,200 Israelis were killed and 240 were taken hostage. The IDF was taken completely by surprise and its lack of preparedness was evident. Israel immediately launched air strikes against Hamas in the Gaza Strip and Netanyahu brought Gantz into his war cabinet, increasing the military expertise he had to hand and reducing the influence of the far-right ministers he had appointed. Several weeks after the attack, Israel launched a ground invasion.

Netanyahu was heavily criticised for his handling of the situation and for his refusal to negotiate a ceasefire that would have precipitated the release of the hostages. Even his own cabinet was critical of his objective of 'total victory'. Poll numbers for him and Likud plummeted as support for Gantz and his National Unity party surged. There was outrage in the international community as the death toll in Gaza mounted and the Israeli prime minister became increasingly isolated. An offensive in May, launched on the city of Rafah – one of the few areas not to have been affected until then by the Israeli response – resulted in a public falling-out with US President Joe Biden. Protests took place in Tel Aviv and Netanyahu was coming under increasing pressure. Towards the end of May, Gantz was threatening to resign if the premier did not deliver a strategy for bringing the conflict to a conclusion. On 20 May, the chief prosecutor of the International Criminal Court announced that he would be seeking arrest warrants for Netanyahu and defence minister, Yoav Gallant (b. 1958), for war crimes, seeking the same for the Hamas leaders, Yahya Sinwar (1962-2024), Ismail Haniyeh

(1962-2024) and Mohammed Deif (1965-2024). Netanyahu was incensed that the actions of the IDF were being seen as equivalent to those of Hamas. The warrants were issued in November, but this action only served to prompt a slight rise in the prime minister's popularity.

Netanyahu insisted in July 2024 that he would only agree to a ceasefire if Israel was permitted to remain in control of the border zone (the Philadelphi Corridor) between the Gaza Strip and Egypt which the IDF had entered in May. On 31 August the bodies of six Israeli hostages who, it transpired, had only been dead for a few days, were recovered. Hundreds of thousands of anguished Israelis took to the streets demanding that Netanyahu make a deal with Hamas for the return of all the hostages still in Gaza, but the prime minister merely repeated his demand regarding the Philadelphi Corridor.

There was little change until Donald Trump, elected president of the United States in November 2024, pressurised Netanyahu and Hamas to arrange a hostage deal before his inauguration on 20 January 2025. Of course, the right-wing members of the Israeli government were aghast at the thought of any deal that precluded the destruction of Hamas but Netanyahu forced the deal into existence. This led to the resignation of the Minister of National Security, Itamar Ben-Gvir (b. 1976), and the removal of his party, Otzma Yehudit (Jewish Power), from the coalition. Bezalel Smotrich (b. 1980), Minister of Finance, and leader of the far-right National Religious Party was only persuaded to remain in the coalition by the prime minister's promises of further intensified action by the IDF in the West Bank and Gaza.

In the middle of March, fighting resumed in Gaza and Gvir and his party returned to the coalition and government. A crisis was building, however, as Netanyahu attempted to sack the head of Shin Bet, the Israeli intelligence agency responsible for the investigation of domestic and government affairs. Once again, this raised questions about the separation of powers, especially as Netanyahu's office was being investigated by this very agency. Thousands of Israelis took to the streets to protest the move.

On 18 March 2025, the Gaza War ceasefire that had been initiated in January, was effectively ended by a surprise attack launched by Israel on the Gaza Strip. It was the day that the prime minister was due to begin testifying in his corruption trial, but the legal process was suspended because of the attack. In May, Netanyahu vowed that Israel will 'take control' of all of Gaza, leading the United Kingdom, France and Canada to attack the escalation of the conflict by Israel, threatening a 'concrete response' if the campaign continued. Meanwhile, on 20 May, aid agencies forecast the deaths of thousands of babies in Gaza if substantial supplies of humanitarian aid were not allowed to enter the region.

Israel and Iran: the 12-Day War

In June 2025, Israel and Iran, mortal enemies since the 1979 Islamic Revolution in Iran, finally went to war with each other. The Islamic right in Iran had long viewed Israel as the 'illegitimate occupier of Muslim land' while refusing to acknowledge its right to exist and Israel's close ties with the West, especially with the United States, added to the atmosphere of hatred and mistrust, leading the Iranian leadership to pledge the destruction of Israel on many occasions. After decades of what had been described as a 'proxy war', the first direct attacks occurred on 1 April 2024 when Israel launched an air strike on the Iranian consulate in the Syrian capital, Damascus, killing two Iranian generals. On 13 April, as was inevitable, Iran retaliated with drone and missile attacks against Israel and the Israeli-occupied Golan Heights. The

Israelis responded six days later with strikes on an air defence radar site near Isfahan in central Iran, although satellite imagery showed that little damage was done to the base. Further attacks by each side occurred in October 2024.

On 13 June 2025, the day after the deadline set by US President Donald Trump for securing a deal to bring a halt to Iran's nuclear ambitions, Israel launched Operation Rising Lion – a series of pre-emptive attacks on dozens of targets across Iran, including nuclear facilities, military bases, infrastructure installations as well as on key senior military personnel. The objective of the operation was to do lasting damage to Iran's nuclear programme amid growing fears that the Iranians were edging closer to making a nuclear weapon. In fact, towards the end of Joe Biden's presidency, US intelligence sources suggested that Iran was just a few months away from having the capability to manufacture such a weapon. The country had increased its uranium enrichment since President Trump, in his first term of office, had withdrawn America from the nuclear deal with Iran – the Joint Comprehensive Plan of Action – that had been negotiated by Barack Obama during his presidency. This withdrawal and a resumption of sanctions took place even though it had been proved that up until this point the Iranians had been sticking to their side of the bargain. But, on 12 June 2025, the International Atomic Energy Agency (IAEA) declared that for the first time in twenty years Iran was non-compliant with its nuclear obligations. That same day, Prime Minister Netanyahu informed President Trump that Israel would attack Iran the following day.

The 13 June attacks were enabled by sabotage of the Iranian air defence system and missile defence infrastructure by Mossad, the Israeli national intelligence agency. A number of senior Iranian military men were assassinated, as well as leaders of the Iranian Revolutionary Guards, nuclear scientists and around

200 civilians. Those parts of the nuclear facility near Natanz that were above ground were destroyed by airstrikes, and the uranium conversion facility at Isfahan was badly damaged. In the afternoon, strikes continued near Tabriz airport and at the Hamadan airbase. However, the vital underground Fordow Fuel Enrichment Plant which also came under attack, remained intact, the Israelis lacking the ordinance to penetrate deep into the ground. Iran responded with missile and drone attacks on US and Israeli forces and military bases across the Middle East. Some missiles struck Tel Aviv, but many were intercepted. There were 63 Israeli casualties, one female civilian later dying of her injuries.

On the ninth day of the conflict, the United States also went on the offensive, bombing three Iranian nuclear sites – Fordow, Natanz and Isfahan – as part of Operation Midnight Hammer. Fourteen so-called 'Bunker-buster' bombs were dropped by Northrop B-2 Spirit stealth bombers while Tomahawk missiles rained in from a submarine positioned offshore. According to the US President, Iran's major nuclear enrichment facilities were 'completely and totally obliterated' and Iran's Foreign Minister, Abbas Araghchi (b. 1962), admitted that nuclear sites had, indeed, been severely damaged. Iran responded by attacking the Al Udeid Air Base in Qatar but without casualties. On 23 June President Trump announced a ceasefire between Iran and Israel that would be fully executed by 25 June, thus giving the conflict its name, the '12-Day War'.

During the war, 657 Iranians died and more than 2,000 were wounded. 28 Israelis died as a result of the Iranian attacks and more than 3,000 were injured. The war rendered the Middle East even more unstable and there is uncertainty about what happens next. Iran may rebuild its nuclear capabilities at the same time as increasing its military strength which will undoubtedly lead to further cycles of strikes, sabotage and sanctions. The danger is escalation into an all-out regional war pulling in many different participants from across the region. Of course, a return to negotiations could happen but the stumbling block of nuclear enrichment remains. The Trump regime demands zero enrichment which is a step too far for Iran. Iran may, on the other hand, decide to go for broke and build a nuclear arsenal but it would be a perilous route to take and would achieve little for the country. Ultimately, though, the Iranians may just decide to wait it out, hoping that America's attention moves elsewhere. They could endure whatever sanctions are thrown their way while strengthening ties with China and Russia and importing defence systems from them. The dangers are immense, but whatever path Iran chooses, there will be major implications for the region and for the entire world.

Israel and Hamas: the Gaza War (June to August 2025)

Meanwhile, Israeli military operations continued in the Gaza Strip following the deadly Hamas attacks of 7 October 2023, with 'targeted ground activities', and airstrikes throughout March and April 2025. There was outrage around the world when United Nations bases, hospitals, civilian buildings and aid centres were struck, killing many civilians. On 4 May, the Israeli security cabinet announced Operation Gideon's Chariots, an expansion of its offensive in Gaza, the principal objective being the destruction of Hamas and the capture of 75 per cent of the region.

By June 2025, much of the Gaza Strip had been razed to the ground and, as we have already seen, a terrible humanitarian crisis was developing with famine looming and the healthcare system in total collapse. Hospitals were evacuated under orders of the IDF and a blockade, tightened by the Israelis at the start of the war, brought significant shortages of food, fuel, water and essential medical supplies. Electricity was in short supply which had an impact on hospitals, sewage plants and the vital desalination plants that provided drinking water for Gazans. Many, including a special committee set up by the United Nations to examine Israel's prosecution of the war, claimed that the Israelis had, in fact, committed genocide against the Palestinian people. More than 63,000 Gazans had died in the fighting, but Hamas continued, nonetheless, to operate in the Gaza Strip, despite the IDF claiming to have occupied much of the area. In fact, Hamas launched a counter-offensive of its own in response to Israel's activity – a series of small-scale actions in an operation named Stones of David.

On 4 August, Israeli sources were reported as saying that the IDF operation had ended and they had indeed succeeded in their aim to control more than 75 per cent of the Gaza Strip. They had failed, however, in their other major objectives – the destruction of Hamas, the recovery of hostages taken on 7 October 2023 and the relocation of the civilian population of Palestine to the southern Gaza Strip. But the Israeli government insisted that operations would continue and on 7 August Netanyahu's cabinet approved plans for the occupation of Gaza City, calling up 60,000 reservists for the beginning of September to help carry out the operation. Netanyahu claimed that the occupation of the city was necessary for Israel to 'finish the job' and finally defeat Hamas but the plan faced criticism by the United Nations, Germany, the President of the European Council, Denmark, the United Kingdom, Turkey, China and Saudi Arabia. United Nations Secretary-General António Guterres warned of 'more death and destruction' while French President Emmanuel Macron said the attack on the city 'can only lead to disaster for both peoples and risks plunging the entire region into a cycle of permanent war'.

On 20 August, Hamas agreed to a peace plan that involved the release of around half of the 20 remaining Israeli hostages still in captivity as well as the bodies of dead hostages in exchange for 150 Palestinians who were being held in Israeli prisons. This would all happen during a proposed 60-day ceasefire. The Israelis, given two days to respond to the proposal, failed to react. That same day, Palestinians began to flee Gaza City as the IDF launched the first stages of its planned ground offensive against the capital of the Gaza Governate with an intensive overnight bombardment. On 25 August, an Israeli air strike hit Nasser Hospital in southern Gaza, killing twenty people, amongst whom were five journalists who worked for Associated Press, Reuters, Al Jazeera and other media companies. The raid took the form of a so-called 'double tap' strike whereby a first strike is followed by another shortly after, hitting first responders and medical personnel on their way to provide aid at the scene of the attack. Many consider this tactic to be a war crime as it contravenes the Geneva Convention. The IDF insisted that 'terrorist activities' against Israeli soldiers had been directed from the hospital using a camera located on the roof while journalists on the ground maintained that the camera was, in fact, owned and operated by the Reuters news agency. Benjamin Netanyahu later expressed regret at the strike.

As August drew to a close, Israeli drones circled over the city, dropping leaflets instructing people to evacuate to south of Wadi Gaza, a valley that bisects the Gaza Strip. Meanwhile, Israel declared Gaza City a 'dangerous combat zone' and thousands of Gazans fled as the Israeli assault intensified. On Saturday 30 August, 77 Gazans died in the city, at least 11 of them, including 3 children, reported to have been gunned down by Israeli soldiers while queuing for food. Hundreds of thousands of people sheltered while hunger and famine grew and Israel began to attack densely populated areas of the city, forcing families to flee and set up tents close to the Nuseirat refugee camp and near Deir al-Balah in Central Gaza. An anonymous Israeli official was reported to have claimed that Israel planned to slow down or even stop the delivery of humanitarian aid in parts of northern Gaza, preventing air drops of aid and deliveries by relief trucks. In Tel Aviv, meanwhile, protestors demanded that the Israeli government should seek a ceasefire rather than escalate its offensive.

Conditions in Gaza were desperate. More than a million people had been displaced in the central and western parts of Gaza City alone. Further restrictions in aid put at risk the lives of countless numbers of Palestinians but, after 700 days of war, as autumn approached, the Israeli onslaught seemed no nearer the end.

Index

9/11, 173-6, 179, 193

Abbasid Dynasty, 36, 38, 40, 44
Abdul Hamid II, Sultan, 75, 82, 84
Abdullah, King of Transjordan, 99, 112, 143
Abraham Accords, 208
Achaemenid Empire, 17, 27
Acre, 42-3, 61
Aden (formerly South Yemen), 77, 91-2, 135, 183
Afghanistan, 9, 87, 134, 161, 174-7, 190-3, 202
Ahmadinejad, Mahmoud, President, 162, 194
Akhund, Hasan, 193
Akhundzada, Hibatullah, 193
Akkadian Empire, 13-7
al-Ahd (Arab nationalist secret society), 91
al-Assad, Bashar, President, 184-5, 188-9
Alawites (Syrian minority), 123, 125, 186, 190
al-Baghdadi, Abu Bakr, 201-2
al-Banna, Hasan, 114, 116
al-Bashir, Mohammed, 189-90

Aleppo, 21, 49, 94, 123, 185, 187, 189
Alexander the Great, 17, 20, 23, 29, 60
Alexandria, 20, 60, 62, 74
al-Fatat (Arab nationalist secret society), 91
al-Hariri, Saad, 197
al-Houthi, Abdul-Malik, 183
al-Houthi, Mohammed Ali, 183
Ali, Muhammad, 61-6, 72, 144
Allied nations, 91, 93-5, 103, 109, 122, 130-2
al-Masri, Abu Ayyub, 201
al-Nusra Front, 188, 201-2
al-Qaeda, 175-6, 190, 200-1
al-Said, Nuri, 143, 151-2
al-Sharaa, Ahmed, 189
al-Zarqawi, Abu Musab, 200
al-Zawahiri, Ayman, Dr, 175, 201
America. *See* United States
Amini, Mahsa, 196
Amorites, 15-6, 21
Anglo-Iranian Oil Company (AIOC), 121, 155
Aoun, Joseph, President, 200
Arab League, 132, 168, 170
Arab Spring, 181

Arab-Israeli War, 113, 139-40
Arafat, Yasser, Palestinian leader, 170, 172
Arg, the, 193
Arif, Abd al-Salam, Colonel, 151-3
Army of Conquest, 187
Assyria, 14, 17, 22-4, 26
Atatürk. *See* Mustafa, Kemal
Augustus, Emperor (Octavian), 20, 30
Austria, 42, 59, 71, 84, 86, 155, 203
Axis nations, 128-32, 179

Ba'ath (Revival) Party, 151-2, 154, 184
Babylon, 10, 15-7, 21, 24, 27, 29, 36
Babylonia, 14-5, 23-4
Babylonian, 15-7, 26-7
Baghdad, 36, 38, 40, 44, 49-50, 83, 95-7, 116-7, 151-2, 166, 180, 202
Baghdadi, Abu Omar, 201
Bahrain, 54, 77, 166, 183
Balfour Declaration, 98-99, 109, 137
Barak, Ehud, Prime Minister, 172
Barzani, Mustafa, 153
Bayezid, son of Murad, 48-9, 53
Begin, Menachem, 169-70
Beirut, 65, 123, 169, 199-200
Beirut explosion, 199
Ben-Gvir, Itamar, 210
Bennett, Naftali, Prime Minister, 208
Bezeq, 207
Biden, Joe, President, 192, 209, 212
bin Laden, Osama, 174-7
bin Salman, Mohammed, Prince, 197
Bonaparte, Napoleon, 60-1
Bush, George HW, President, 167
Bush, George W, President, 177, 179-80

Byzantine Empire, 10, 35, 39-40, 47-9

Caesar, Julius, Roman general, 29-30
Cairo, 38, 60-2, 101, 130, 145, 182
Cambyses II, King, 20, 28
Camp David, 149, 169-70, 172
Canada, 158, 183, 211
Capitulations, 57, 66, 72, 80, 114
Carter, Jimmy, President, 159, 161, 169-70
Carthage, 22-3
chemical weapons, 164, 178, 180, 186, 188, 202
China, 38, 49, 86-7, 194, 214-5
Churchill, Winston, Prime Minister, 111, 130, 156
CIA, Central Intelligence Agency, 156-7, 161, 180
CID, Criminal Investigation Department, 137
Clinton, Bill, President, 170-2
Constantine the Great, 33
Constantinople, 35, 39, 42, 48-50, 57, 95-6, 102
Corruption Perceptions Index, 193
COVID-19, 195, 198, 207
Crimean War, 69-71
Cromer, Lord, 77-9
Crusades, the, 40-1, 43-5, 57
CUP, Committee of Union and Protest, 84-5, 103
Cyrus the Great, 17, 22, 27

D'Arcy, William Knox, 87, 132
Daesh. *See* Islamic State
Dahieh, 200
Damascus, 21, 36, 41, 49, 59, 83, 94, 98-9, 112, 123-4, 184, 186,

INDEX

188-9, 211
Daraa, 184-5, 188-9
Deif, Mohammed, 210
Deir ez-Zour, 188
Diab, Hassan, 198-9
Douma, 188
Druze (Syrian minority), 57, 123, 125, 168, 186

Egypt, 9-10, 17-20, 22, 24-6, 28-30, 33, 35-6, 38-40, 43-4, 50-1, 57, 59-67, 72-3, 77-9, 81, 92, 101-2, 106-8, 113-14, 116, 128-30, 132, 134-5, 141-9, 151, 154, 163, 166, 169-70, 173, 181-3, 204-5, 210
Eisenhower, Dwight D, President, 145-7, 156
Erez Crossing, 205
Eritrea, 128, 202
European Union (EU), 173, 186, 202-3

Faisal, Amir, 92-3, 98-9, 117-8, 122
Farouk, King of Egypt, 114, 129-30, 142, 144-5
Fatah, 172-3, 205
Fatimid Dynasty, 38, 40-1
fellahin (peasants), 64, 106, 118, 144
First World War, 9, 79, 84, 87, 91-101, 103, 108, 119, 122, 128, 132
France, 10, 38, 42, 57, 59-62, 65, 70-1, 77, 83-4, 96-8, 101-2, 104, 107, 112, 122-6, 128-9, 146, 166, 177, 180, 183, 194, 211
Free Officers Movement, 144
Free Syrian Army, 185, 187

Gallant, Yoav, 209
Gallipoli Campaign, 95

Gantz, Benny, 207, 209
Gaza Strip, 94, 141, 148, 171-3, 199, 205, 209-11, 214-7
Germany, 61, 83-4, 93-4, 109, 121, 177, 180, 183, 203, 215
Ghani, Ashraf, President, 191-3
Golan Heights, 148-9, 188, 206, 211
Great Britain, 10, 59-61, 65, 70-1, 77, 79-80, 83-4, 88, 91, 96-9, 101-2, 104, 106-8, 112-3, 119-22, 128-30, 136-7, 140, 144-6, 150, 155-6, 166, 179-80, 186, 203
Gulf War, First, 165-6, 175, 177

Hadith, 34
Ham, 189
Hamas, 171-3, 189, 199, 205, 209-10, 214-6
Hamid Karzai International Airport, 193
Hammurabi, King of Babylon, 10, 15-6
Haniyeh, Ismail, 209
Haredi Judaism, 207
Hayat Tahrir al-Sham (HTS), 187-9
Helmand, 192
Hezbollah, 162, 172, 186, 189, 197-200
Hittites, 16, 19-23
Holy Land, 40, 42, 70
Homs, 123, 185-6, 188-9
Hungary, 48, 50, 84, 147, 203
Hussein, Saddam, 152-4, 162, 180

Ibrahim, son of Muhammad Ali, 64-5
Idlib, 187-9
International Atomic Energy Agency (IAEA), 195, 212
International Criminal Court, 209

International Monetary Fund (IMF), 193, 199
Iran, 9, 14, 16, 24, 36-7, 43, 53, 55, 75, 77, 79-81, 87-9, 93, 101, 116-7, 119-22, 128, 132, 134, 153-66, 179, 186-9, 194-7, 204, 211-4
Iran-Iraq War, 161-164
Iraq, 9, 30, 36-7, 84, 91-3, 97, 101-2, 105, 116-8, 129, 132-5, 141, 143, 150-4, 159, 161-7, 177-81, 186, 191, 200-2
Irgun (Jewish terrorist group), 136-8
Iron Dome, 205
ISIS. *See* Islamic State
Islamic State (ISIL), 187-8, 190-1, 200 2
Ismail the Magnificent, 72, 79
Israel, 9, 24-6, 108, 111, 113, 140-1, 145-6, 148-51, 154, 157, 160, 163-4, 167-73, 188-9, 198-200, 205-17
Israel Hayom, 207
Israel-Hamas War, 204-210, 213-216
Israeli Defence Force (IDF), 141, 168, 205, 209-10, 214-6
Israeli High Court of Justice, 208
Istanbul, 39, 50, 67, 83-5, 91, 101, 103-5

Janissaries, 48, 51, 66
Jericho, 10, 141
Jerusalem, 26, 30-1, 41-2, 137-8, 141, 148, 154, 163, 172, 206
Jesus Christ, 31, 33-4, 41
Jewish Agency, the, 136-8
Jewish Home, 206
Jewish National Home, 111-2, 136
jihad (holy war), 41, 174-5
Joint Comprehensive Plan of Action, 195, 212
Jordan, 9, 99, 112-3, 136, 141, 143, 148, 152, 171, 181, 183, 186, 204
Judah, Kingdom of, 24, 26-7

Kabul, 191, 193
Kamel, Hussein, 79, 106
Kemal, Mustafa, 74, 95, 103-5
Khamenei, Ali, Supreme Leader, 162, 195-6
Khan Shaykhūn, 188
khedive (viceroy), 72-3, 78-9, 106
Khomeini, Ruhollah, Ayatollah, 158-63, 165
Kitchener, Herbert, General, 79, 91
Koran, 34, 37, 114
Kulanu, 206
Kunduz, 192
Kurdistan Workers' Party (PKK), 190
Kurds, 37, 117, 153-4, 165, 186, 189-90, 197
Kuwait, 77, 135, 164-7, 177, 181, 183, 203

League of Nations, 101, 107, 122, 124
Lebanon, 9, 22, 29, 57, 65, 94, 101-2, 112-3, 122-3, 125-6, 129, 132, 134-5, 141, 143, 161-2, 167-70, 172, 186, 189, 197-200, 204
Levant, the, 9, 16, 18, 21-2, 24, 122, 200-1
Libya, 19, 28, 128, 135, 181, 202
Likud, 169, 207, 209

Macron, Emmanuel, President, 199, 215
Mahdi, Muhammad Ahmad, 78
Mahmud II, Sultan, 65-6, 68

INDEX

Majlis, the (Iranian parliament), 88, 195
Mamlukes, 43-5, 57, 60, 62
Mandate, 94, 97-9, 102, 110-2, 116, 122, 124-6, 134, 137-8, 140-1
March 14 Bloc, 197-8
March 8 Bloc, 197
Maronite, 122-3, 125-6, 168
Mecca, 35, 50, 64, 91, 99
Medes, 24, 27
Medina, 64, 83, 92
Mehmed II, Sultan, 49
Mehmed VI, Sultan, 103-4
Mikati, Najib, Prime Minister, 199
Mongols, the, 43-4, 47
Moors, the, 10, 41
Morocco, 50, 77, 135, 181, 183
Mosaddegh, Mohammed, 155-7, 161
Moses, 34
Mubarak, Hosni, President, 182
Muhammad, the Prophet, 34-5
mujahideen, 174-5
Murad, grandson of Osman, 48
Muslim Brotherhood (Society of Muslim Brothers), 114, 116, 144-5, 174
Mustafa, Kemal, 103, 105

Naguib, Muhammad, first president of Egypt, 144-5
Nasrallah, Hassan, 200
Nasser, Gamal Abdel, 144-9
National Pact, 104-5
National Unity, 148, 173, 198, 207, 209
NATO, 191
Netanyahu, Benjamin, Prime Minister, 206-12, 215-6
New York City, 176, 190

Nixon, Richard, President, 149, 159
North Waziristan, 191
nuclear weapons / warfare / programme, 149, 162, 177-9, 194-5, 212-4

Obama, Barack, President, 202, 212
oil interests / reserves / facilities, 87-8, 93, 95, 97, 117-20, 128, 132-3, 136, 146, 150-3, 156, 158-62, 164-7, 174, 178, 195
Oman, 135, 166, 183
OPEC, Organisation of Petroleum Exporting Companies, 158, 165
Operation Decisive Storm, 183
Operation Enduring Freedom, 177, 190
Operation Protective Edge, 205
Operation Restoring Hope, 183
Operation Triton, 203
Orthodox Judaism, 207
Oslo Accords, 171
Osman, 47-8
Ottoman Empire, 9-10, 47-53, 57-62, 64-72, 74-5, 77, 79-84, 86-7, 91-9, 101-5, 111, 116, 122, 124, 128, 132
Otzma Yehudit, 210

Pahlavi, Reza, Shah of Iran, 119-20, 122
Pakistani militants, 191
Palestine Liberation Organisation (PLO), 136, 150, 168, 170-2
Palestinian Authority, 171
Palestinian Islamic Jihad (PIJ), 205
Pan-Islamism, 82-3
Parthians, 17, 29-30
Peres, Shimon, Prime Minister, 171

Pezeshkian, Masoud, President, 197
Philadelphi Corridor, 210
Phoenicians, 22-3
Prigozhin, Yevgeny, 187
Ptolemaic Empire, 20, 29
Putin, Vladimir, President, 187

Qajar Dynasty, 79-80, 119-20
Qasim, Adb al-Karim, Brigadier-General, 151-2
Qatar, 166, 183, 186, 213

Rabin, Yitzhak, Prime Minister, 150, 171
Rafah, 205, 209
Rafah Crossing, 205
Raisi, Ebrahim, President, 195-7
Ramesses II, the Great, 19, 21
Raqqa, 187-8
Reagan, Ronald, President, 161-2, 164, 170
Red Sea, the, 30, 38, 51, 92, 183
Refugee Crisis, 201-203
Revolutionary Command Council, 187
Revolutionary Guards, 196, 212
Roman Empire, 20, 26, 29-31, 33, 39
Rouhani, Hassan, President, 162, 194-6
Russia, 52, 58-61, 65, 70-1, 80-1, 84, 87-8, 93-4, 96, 108, 120-2, 132, 173, 180, 187, 189, 214

Sadat, Anwar, President, 130, 144, 149, 154, 169-70
Safavid Dynasty, 50, 52-5, 58, 79-80
Saladin, 41-3
Samuel, Herbert, Sir, 110-2
San Remo Conference, 97-8, 112

Saudi Arabia, 64, 101, 132, 134-5, 143, 164, 166, 174-5, 182-3, 186, 197, 215
SAVAK (National Intelligence and Security Organisation, Iran), 157, 159
Schengen Agreement, 203
Seleucid Empire, 17, 29-30
Selim III, 59, 67
Seljuks, 40-1, 43-4
Semitic, 15, 19, 22, 30
Serbia, 49, 71, 86, 203
Sèvres, Treaty of, 98, 103-4
Shariah, 34, 69, 72, 81, 85, 88, 99, 116, 121, 201
Shas, 206
Shayrat, 188
Shi'ism, 53, 88
Shia, 35, 53-4, 80, 180, 186, 200
Shiite, 36, 38, 80, 150-1, 153, 162, 167-8
Shin Bet, 210
Sidqi, Ismail, Prime Minister, 142
Sinai Peninsula, 141, 148
Sinwar, Yahya, 209
Smotrich, Bezalel, 210
Stern Group, 136
Sudan, Republic of, 19, 28, 63-5, 77-9, 107, 114, 135, 142-3, 175-6, 181, 183
Suez Canal, 73, 83, 92, 94-5, 113-4, 144-7
Suez Crisis, 74, 144-147
Suleiman the Magnificent, 50, 182
Sumer, 13-5, 27
Sunnah, 34, 114
Sunni, 35-6, 54, 57, 64, 117-8, 123, 125-6, 135, 152, 162, 167, 180, 186-7, 200-1

INDEX

Sweden, 203
Sykes-Picot Agreement, 96, 107
Syria, 9, 14-5, 17, 19, 21-3, 25, 29-31, 35-41, 43-4, 49-50, 61, 65, 84, 91-4, 97-9, 101-2, 107, 112, 116-7, 122-6, 129, 132, 134, 141, 143, 147-8, 151, 154, 166, 168, 170, 172, 184-91, 200, 202, 204
Syrian Interim Government, 187
Syrian Salvation Government, 188-9

Taliban, 176-7, 191-4
Tanzimat (reforms), 68-9, 74, 82
Teheran, 80, 88, 101, 120, 122, 153, 155, 159-60, 164
Tel Aviv, 137, 200, 209, 213, 217
Tewfik, 73-4
Thrace, 28, 86, 93, 97, 103
ThyssenKrupp, 207
Time, 191
Timur, Central Asian warlord, 48-9, 52
Transjordan, 99, 101, 112, 132, 134, 141, 143
Tripoli, 41, 77, 86, 123
Truman, Harry S, President, 137, 154-6
Trump, Donald, President, 190-1, 195, 206, 210, 212-4
Turkey, 9, 14, 20-1, 36-7, 43, 69-70, 83-4, 86-7, 91, 95, 101, 103-5, 117, 125, 128, 134-5, 143, 166, 185-9, 204, 215
Tyre, 17, 22-3, 123

Ukraine, 20, 189, 191, 196
ulama (religious elite), 66-7, 69, 80-1, 99, 116
Umayyad Caliphate, 10

United Arab Emirates, 183
United Kingdom, 158, 177, 183, 191, 194, 211, 215
United National Front (UNF), 151-2
United Nations, 134, 139-42, 150, 165-7, 173, 177-80, 183, 186, 191, 202, 204-5, 214-5
United Nations Humanitarian Relief (UNHCR), 204
United States, 108-10, 118, 131, 143, 145-7, 149-50, 156-66, 170, 175-7, 179-81, 183, 186-95, 201, 203, 206, 208, 210-4
United Torah Judaism, 206
Urabi, Ahmed (Urabi Revolt), 73-4
Uzbek militants, 53
Uzbeks, 53-4

Wafd Party (Egypt), 113-4, 130, 142-3
Wagner Group, 187
Wallachia, 48-9, 70
weapons of mass destruction (WMDs), 177-80
Weizmann, Chaim, Dr, 108-10
West Bank, 141, 148, 171-3, 208, 210
World Bank, 193
World Trade Center, 176, 190

Yamkhad, 21, 23
Yedioth Ahronoth, 207
Yemen, 92, 101, 134-5, 175, 181-3, 191
Yom Kippur War (Ramadan War), 149, 158
Young Turks, 75, 84, 92

Zaghloul, Saad, 106, 113-4
Zionists, 98, 108-11, 136-40, 150

OLDCASTLE BOOKS

POSSIBLY THE UK'S SMALLEST INDEPENDENT PUBLISHING GROUP

Oldcastle Books is an independent publishing company formed in 1985 dedicated to providing an eclectic range of titles with a nod to the popular culture of the day.

Imprints include our lists about the film industry, KAMERA BOOKS & CREATIVE ESSENTIALS. We have dabbled in the classics, with PULP! THE CLASSICS, taken a punt on gambling books with HIGH STAKES, provided in-depth overviews with POCKET ESSENTIALS and covered a wide range in the eponymous OLDCASTLE BOOKS list. Most recently we have welcomed two new sister imprints with THE CRIME & MYSTERY CLUB and VERVE, home to great, original, page-turning fiction.

oldcastlebooks.com

OLDCASTLE BOOKS		CREATIVE ESSENTIALS		THE CRIME & MYSTERY CLUB
POCKET ESSENTIALS		PULP! THE CLASSICS		VERVE BOOKS
KAMERA BOOKS		HIGHSTAKES PUBLISHING		